Microsoft®
Excel for Office 365
Beginning
Instructor Guide

COPYRIGHT

TRADEMARKS

DISCLAIMER

Product Code: MS EXCEL FOR OFFICE 365-1 GUIDE 19.1

TABLE OF CONTENTS

DEVELOPMENT PHILOSOPHY

As an experienced instructor, you have probably taught from many training manuals, each developed/written in a different manner. Each developer has a distinct way of approaching a class and we are, of course, no different.

Our number one concern is to return control of the classroom to the <u>instructor</u>. Most of the training manuals written are oriented towards a "tutorial" format, requiring the instructor to strictly follow a script. If you deviate from the script or skip a section, the end results do not always match the exercise, which throws the students off. Or the follow-up exercises depended on you completing the previous exercise exactly as specified in order to work.

As a result, the trainer simply becomes a "reader" - meaning you end up reading the exercise almost word-for-word to the student. As long as students can read, they really don't need you unless <u>they</u> deviate from the script and get into trouble.

If you do skip a section or change things around, students get irritated because "that's not the way it is in the book!" Your class is actually being taught by the training manual and <u>not</u> by you!

We believe that **you**, not the manual should be controlling the flow of the class. After all, you are the professional being paid for the training! Every experienced instructor has their own way of teaching a class. You know what exercises are good examples, when to give them and how long to spend on a topic. If a class is slower or faster, you can sense that and can give more exercises as needed or maybe spend a little more time on a topic if the class is a bit slower.

Our courseware is written in the form of a "reference" manual - meaning that the students can use the manual when they return to work/home as a reference rather than a step-by-step tutorial.

Think back for a moment to one of your recent classes where you were teaching from a tutorial manual. Remember that student sitting in the back, not paying attention to a single word you were saying? What was he/she doing? They were reading ahead in the manual, doing every little step in the book as fast as they could read and type! They were so pleased with themselves that they could "read" how to do this program that they missed out on all your great examples, tricks/shortcuts and additional explanations! This happens all of the time with scripted courses. These people don't really learn this way, they just blindly type in commands, not really understanding what they are doing.

This is only one of the many problems that you run into with "tutorial" courseware, but let's focus on the advantages of using our manuals.

ADVANTAGES

There are several advantages to using this format which we have broken down according to three basic categories: students; instructors; and clients.

Advantages for the Student

➢ It's an easy-to-read reference guide. If a student needs to know how to do something, they don't have to read through pages and pages of "Johnny's" letter to mom to figure it out!

Once students leave your class and are dependent upon themselves, they need something that they can use to quickly look up a command or function. Our manual discusses each major topic on a separate page in an easy-to-follow format.

➢ Student notes are in the same book - not written on some pad of paper that they just grabbed for class and will misplace later! How many times have you seen students leave their notes in class after writing down all of the information? But how many manuals are left behind?

The left page of our manual is set aside for the student to be able to write down in their own words what they understand and also any additional information that you might be giving. And it can be written right across from the page of the topic actually being referred to, making it easy to refer back to once class has ended.

➢ Each course can be tailored to the class. Some of the sample exercises in tutorials are so boring or have absolutely nothing in common with the client. Without predefined exercises, you can tailor the course to the client using your examples that you have developed over the years.

Advantages for the Instructor

> Students pay attention. Since they do not really know what you are going to be doing next, students have to follow your instructions. This keeps you in control of the class instead of having students in different parts of the book.

> You can alter the speed of the course as required. As you know, each class progresses differently depending on the various experience levels of the students. If you find you have a faster group, you can give additional exercises or go into more depth for each topic. If you have a slower class, you are not pressured into having to complete all of the "scenarios" or "practice" exercises if you feel you cannot cover them adequately.
>
> Again, <u>you</u> are in control. You can speed up or slow the class down as you see fit. You can expand or condense the amount of information covered on a topic as required.

> You can customize your courses without having to do all the development work! Simply change the exercises to topics that relate more closely to the client. This makes them feel as if you are "customizing" the course for them! We have supplied all of our exercise pages in a separate "Files" folder which may be modified and included with the manuals as the training company sees fit.

Advantages for the Client

> ➤ The client is assured of having qualified instructors. Since there are no step-by-step "follow me" type instructions, the instructor must really know the material. How many times have you heard from other instructors how they "winged" it through class by reading the manual? It doesn't take much for someone who does not know the program well to still "teach" a course if they have a step-by-step tutorial to follow!
>
> Would you send that instructor to one of <u>your</u> clients?

> ➤ More productive employees. Since students <u>actually</u> have to pay attention, students absorb more of what they do.
>
> Since the class can be customized, the client can be sure that students are learning exactly what they need in order to perform their jobs more efficiently once they return to their workplace.

HOW TO USE THIS MANUAL

This manual was designed to be used as a reference. This is not a step-by-step tutorial. Our feeling is that you did not pay to have someone stand in front of class and <u>read</u> you something that you could do on your own. Through our own classroom experience, we have discovered that students don't read detailed descriptions and that lengthy text is ignored. They prefer to explore and try things out.

In typical tutorials, students often get lost following rote procedures and get caught in error conditions from which they can't back out of. Besides, once students leave class, they just want something they can use to look up a subject quickly without having to read through an entire tutorial.

Our design ensures that each course is stimulating and customized yet covers the outlined objectives. Keys that you need to press are displayed as icons such as ENTER or ⬆.

Each topic starts on a new page, making things easy to find and follow. In addition, topics covering actual commands always begin with the USAGE section where we explain the purpose of the command.

The next page shows how a typical topic will be discussed and each part found in the book.

THE TOPIC TITLE WILL BE ON TOP

USAGE: This part of the manual explains what the command is used for, how it works and other miscellaneous information.

This icon indicates tools or buttons to click on with your mouse.

This part lists the keystrokes and function keys the user may press as a shortcut way of performing the command.

Microsoft Excel supports a whole host of touch-screen gestures, including the swiping, pinching and rotating motions familiar to smartphone and tablet users. Tapping an item opens it; pressing and holding an item pops up a menu to display more information about it (similar to [RIGHT] clicking). This icon indicates a touch-screen gesture.

NOTE:	*This box will tell of things to watch out for. The symbol in the left column always indicates an important note to remember.*

TIP:	*This box will let you in on a little secret or shortcut when working with Excel. When you see this icon, you'll know that a "TIP is available.*

Module One

- **Spreadsheet Basics**
- **The Excel Screen**
- **Movement Keys**
- **Accessing Help**

SPREADSHEET BASICS

A spreadsheet is the computerized equivalent of a general ledger. It has taken the place of the pencil, paper and calculator. Spreadsheet programs were first developed for accountants but have now been adopted by anyone wanting to prepare a budget, forecast sales data, create profit and loss statements, compare financial alternatives, and any other mathematical applications requiring calculations.

The electronic spreadsheet is laid out similar to the paper ledger sheet in that it is divided into columns and rows. Any task that can be done on paper can be performed on an electronic spreadsheet faster and more accurately.

The problem with manual sheets is that if any error is found within the data, all answers must be erased and recalculated manually. With the computer, formulas can be written that are automatically updated whenever the data is changed. By having formulas that automatically recalculate, you can play with the numbers to see how the final result is affected.

The horizontal bar across the top of the worksheet is filled with letters, beginning with A and ending with the letter XFD. Each letter represents a **column** while the vertical bar along the left side of the worksheet is filled with numbers that refer to **rows**. The rows are numbered 1 through 1048576.

The intersection between a column and a row is referred to as a **cell**. A cell is similar to a box that can be used to store pieces of information. Each piece of information could be a word or group of words, a number or a mathematical formula.

Each cell has its own **address**. This address is used in formulas for referencing different parts of the worksheet. The address of a cell is defined by the letter of the column it is located in and the number of the row. For example, the address of a cell in column B, row 5 would be referred to as **B5**. The column is always listed first followed by the row without any spaces between the two.

These cell addresses are useful when entering formulas. Instead of typing actual values in your equations, you simply type the cell address that the value is stored in. Then, if you need to go back and change one of the values the spreadsheet automatically updates the answer based on the new number(s).

For example, instead of typing 67*5.4 you could enter C5*D5. The number 67 is stored in cell C5 and the number 5.4 is stored in cell D5. If these numbers change next month or next year, the formula remains correct as it references the cells - not the actual values. With the second formula, you can change the numbers stored in cells C5 and D5 as often as required and see the result recalculate immediately.

RUNNING MICROSOFT EXCEL

USAGE:

Microsoft Excel can be accessed through the Start menu, the Windows desktop or the taskbar (located along the bottom of the desktop window).

If you have pinned a shortcut to your desktop, click or tap the **Excel** icon to run the application.

If you have pinned it to your taskbar, simply click on the Excel icon:

If Excel isn't located on the desktop or taskbar, you'll need to display all of your apps (from within the Start menu).

Open the Start menu.

Instructor Note:

After offering a brief overview of the features within Excel, have students access the program through the Start menu.

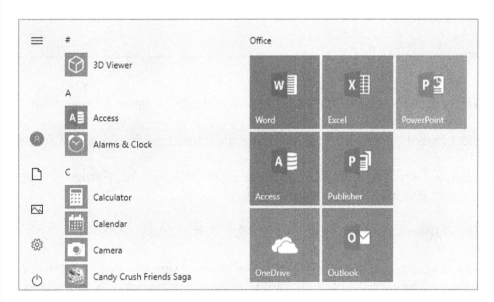

If it isn't already pinned to the Start menu (along the right), scroll through the alphabetical listing of installed apps or click on a letter to display an alphabetical index where you can quickly get to the app based on the first letter of its name.

THE EXCEL SCREEN

When you first run Excel, the following screen will be displayed:

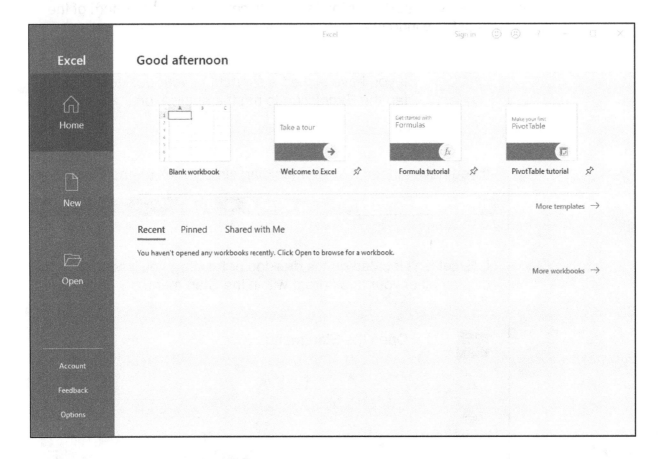

Use **Home** to quickly create a new workbook or open a recent file.

Use **New** to scroll through all of the templates available within Excel.

Notice there are several categories of templates (i.e., Family budget, Project timeline, Back to School Planner, Student schedule).

Use **Open** to browse your system for an existing workbook.

Once you select an item from the left panel, use the right portion of the window to choose the type of new workbook you want to open, or create a new workbook - either a blank one or a new file based on one of the many templates available within Excel.

The screen can be quite intimidating the first time you see it as there are so many items displayed. However, if you take a few minutes to familiarize yourself with the various screen elements, the program will become easier to work with.

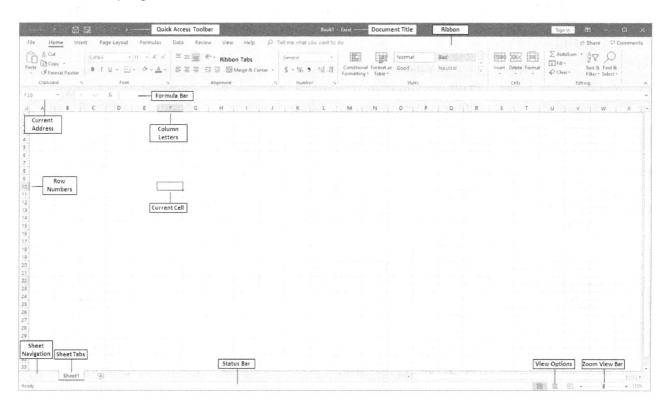

Along the top left corner of the screen is Save tool as well as the Undo and Redo tools.

Since those are tools that are most often used, they are placed in a convenient location on what is referred to as the "Quick Access Toolbar".

Click or tap on the button to the right of these tools ⯆ to customize this Quick Access Toolbar.

The name of current workbook followed by the application name is displayed in the middle. A generic name is given to each new workbook you create (**Book1**).

The right side of the title bar contains an option to sign in to your Microsoft Office account as well as the Ribbon Display Options button ⬆ and three icons for minimizing, maximizing, and closing the program:

⬆	—	🗗	✕

Share	This icon (on the next line) allows you to work with others simultaneously on a file. Click on it to quickly share the current workbook. It also offers live document collaboration to view edits made by other users as they happen.
Comments	This icon allows you to view and respond to comments.

Instructor Note:

This screen will take several minutes to discuss in detail – do not go too quickly over each of the sections.

*However, do point out the **Tell me** search bar which will be discussed in further detail in a few pages. This expanded help feature is a new feature within Office 365 so needs to be discussed.*

The second line contains tabs which are used to access a series of **Ribbons** to help you quickly find the commands needed to complete a task. Commands are organized in logical groups that are collected together under these tabs. Each tab relates to a type of activity, i.e., the View tab contains tools to customize the view.

The last item on the ribbon (a magnifying glass with the words "***Tell me what you want to do..***") is an expansive help feature, offering immediate access to functions and actions within Excel.

To collapse the ribbon, press CTRL+F1. Press CTRL+F1 a second time to display the ribbon again. Even while collapsed, clicking or tapping on a tab will display the ribbon for that tab.

Touch screen users can also display an additional set of commonly used buttons down the right side of the screen (on what is referred to as the **Touch Bar**). To display the Touch Bar, click or tap on ▼ (on the Quick Access Toolbar) and select Touch/Mouse Mode from the pull-down menu. This will also increase the space between buttons on the ribbon.

Along the right side of the screen is the **scroll bar** used to quickly move (vertically) within your workbook. Use the arrows located across the top and bottom of the scrollbar to move up and down.

To move more quickly, drag the small rectangle located within the scroll bar to the desired location (up or down). If you zoom to a larger size than can fit horizontally within the window, a horizontal scroll bar will appear across the bottom of the screen.

The next section across the top of the screen lists the columns and rows within the current worksheet. Columns are lettered and rows are numbered. The first 26 columns are lettered A through Z. Excel then begins lettering the 27th column with AA and so on. In a single Excel worksheet there are 16,384 columns (lettered A-XFD) and 1,048,576 rows (numbered 1-1048576).

The highlighted borders around the workbook window indicate the columns and rows and are used to identify where on the workbook you are located since you obviously cannot see an entire workbook of this size on the screen at one time.

The workbook is located to the right and beneath the borders. This is where you will actually be working and entering information. The outlined cell (the one with the dark borders) within the workbook is referred to as the **active cell**. Each cell may contain text, numbers or dates. You can enter up to 32,767 characters in each cell.

Instructor Note:

Because workbooks are so large, it's important that students know how to easily navigate through them.

Take your time when discussing the layout of the spreadsheet as many users, even those who have worked with Excel for year, don't fully understand its capabilities.

Towards the bottom of the worksheet is a small **Tab** that identifies each sheet within the workbook (file). If there are multiple sheets, you can use the tabs to easily identify what data is stored on each sheet. For example, the top sheet could be "Expenses" and the second sheet could be called "Income". When you begin a new workbook, the tabs default to being labeled **Sheet1, Sheet2**, etc.

Along the bottom of the screen is another bar called the **Status Bar**. This bar is used to display various information about the system and current workbook. The left corner of this line lists the **Mode Indicator** which tells you what mode you are currently working in. When Excel is ready for you to enter text, the mode indicator will read "Ready".

Just below and to the left of the vertical scroll bar is the **Zoom** section. Notice you can click or tap the increase **+** or decrease **-** buttons to change the zoom factor. You can also drag the slider horizontally to change the text size as it appears on the screen. Excel displays the current percentage just to the left of this area.

There is also a section labeled **Zoom** on the View Ribbon across the top of your screen which allows you to customize the display size. This section is used to either open a dialog box where you can choose an exact zoom factor, switch back to 100% zoom (which is the default) or zoom in to the current selection. The last option can be useful when working with a block of cells and wanting to only view them as you work.

To the left of the zoom area located along the bottom of your screen are three **View Icons**. These are used to change the current display (Normal, Page Layout, and Page Break Preview). Simply click on the view you want to switch to.

To make working with multiple workbooks less confusing, Excel has included a feature which automatically displays all opened workbooks along the taskbar. Rather than having to access the Ribbon labeled **View** to switch between opened files (windows), you can simply use your mouse to click on the name of the file you want to access directly on the taskbar. Once selected, that file becomes the active window.

NAVIGATING WITHIN A WORKSHEET

USAGE:

Excel offers both keyboard and mouse methods for moving:

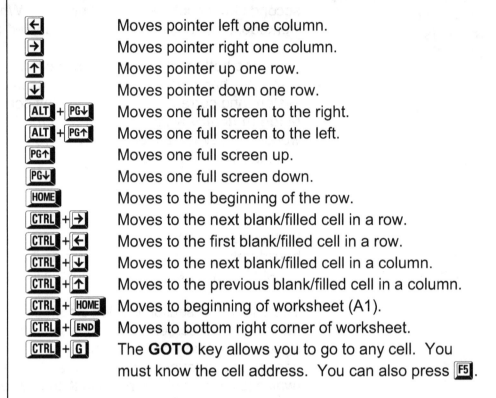

Key	Action
←	Moves pointer left one column.
→	Moves pointer right one column.
↑	Moves pointer up one row.
↓	Moves pointer down one row.
ALT + PG↓	Moves one full screen to the right.
ALT + PG↑	Moves one full screen to the left.
PG↑	Moves one full screen up.
PG↓	Moves one full screen down.
HOME	Moves to the beginning of the row.
CTRL + →	Moves to the next blank/filled cell in a row.
CTRL + ←	Moves to the first blank/filled cell in a row.
CTRL + ↓	Moves to the next blank/filled cell in a column.
CTRL + ↑	Moves to the previous blank/filled cell in a column.
CTRL + HOME	Moves to beginning of worksheet (A1).
CTRL + END	Moves to bottom right corner of worksheet.
CTRL + G	The **GOTO** key allows you to go to any cell. You must know the cell address. You can also press F5.

Click or tap in this box and type the cell address you want to go to. You must press ENTER when done.

You can also use the vertical (down the right) and the horizontal (along the bottom) scroll bars to move. Drag the box in the scroll bar to move more quickly. You must click or tap in a cell to actually move to it. Remember to look at the formula bar across the top of your screen for the current cell address.

If you are using a mouse with a scroll wheel, roll the rubber wheel (located between the **[LEFT]** and **[RIGHT]** mouse buttons) forward or back to quickly scroll through large worksheets.

Excel highlights column and row headings as you move from cell to cell. This helps to distinguish the current cell address.

CHANGING THE WORKBOOK VIEW

USAGE:

By default, you are placed in "Normal" view which simply displays the workbook. However, if you'd prefer to see the headers, footers, and rulers you can switch to "Page Layout" view. To see exactly where page breaks will occur when printing, switch to "Page Break Preview".

To switch between the views, click on one of the following tools (located along the bottom right side of your screen or within the "Workbook Views" section on the View Ribbon):

This tool displays **Normal** view.

This tool displays **Page Layout** view.

This tool displays **Page Break Preview**.

In addition to the three views discussed above, you can create your own custom views (discussed in the advanced manual).

Custom
Views

To switch to a **Custom View**, click or tap on this tool (located within the "Workbook Views" section on the "View" Ribbon). A small dialog box will open allowing you to choose from a list of saved views.

Instructor Note:

Go over each of the view options and allow students to click on the various icons to see for themselves the difference between them.

SHOWING/HIDING SCREEN ITEMS

There is a section on the View Ribbon labeled **Show** that can be used to display or hide screen elements (these include the Ruler, Gridlines, Formula Bar, and Headings).

When checked, the item is displayed and when left unchecked, the item is hidden.

WORKING WITH HELP

USAGE:

Excel offers extensive Help without you having to do more than enter the item you need help on.

Using the **Tell me what you want to do** search bar, you can enter the function or feature you're looking for and Excel will offer you the function itself (rather than a help page describing it).

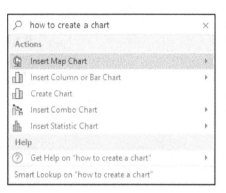

Click or tap in this section (located to the right of the ribbons) and type your question.

As soon as you begin typing, Excel will display help on that topic.

If Excel finds the related commands for that topic, it displays them in the pull-down menu.

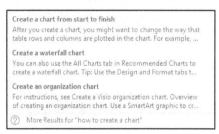

If none of the commands listed are what you want, click on the "Get Help on…" item for an additional menu containing more detailed information on the topic you are searching for.

Use the "Smart Lookup" option (from within the original menu) to search the Internet for topics related to the topic you are currently searching.

Instructor Note:

*It's important that students feel comfortable accessing Help when you are not there (and the **Tell me** search bar is a new feature in Office 365) so take your time with this section.*

Clicking on one of the items within the "Get Help on …" submenu displays a new panel along the right side of your screen:

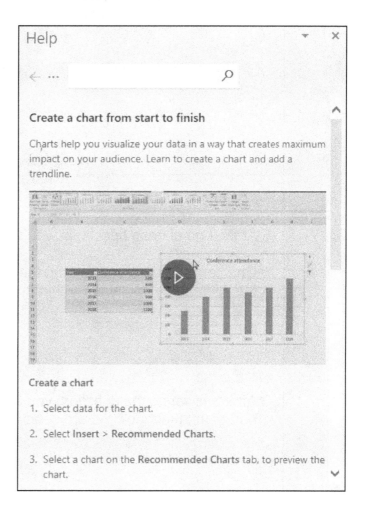

This panel displays help on the item you selected.

Scroll through the step-by-step instructions and diagrams.

The article may include links to related help topics. Some links may require Internet access as they will attempt to launch your Internet browser and access Microsoft's support website.

←   Click on this arrow to return to the previous help screen.

...   Click on the three dots (…) to display a pull-down menu with the following items:

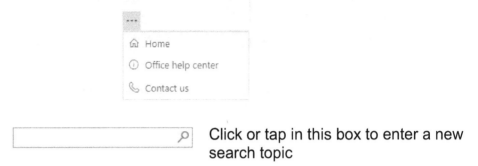

Click or tap in this box to enter a new search topic

At the end of each help topic, you will see two items:

One item will allow you to send feedback to Microsoft as to whether the information contained within the help panel was helpful:

Was this information helpful?

Yes	No

After answering the question, you can also include a comment as part of the feedback you are sending Microsoft:

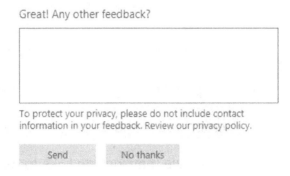

The second item (at the bottom of the help panel) allows you to launch your Internet browser and view more detailed information on the currently selected topic through Microsoft's support website:

Read article in browser ⧉

You can then use your browser's print option if you'd like to print out information on the selected topic.

EXITING HELP

✖   Click or tap this button (located in the top right corner) to **close** the help window and return to your workbook.

SCREENTIPS

A common problem most users encounter is not knowing what each tool on the screen represents.

For example, the SAVE tool is displayed as a 3.5" diskette which some users do not immediately relate to saving a file.

To alleviate this problem, Excel offers quick mouse assistance on each tool, referred to as ScreenTips.

As you point to a tool, Excel will display a quick note as to the tool's function.

Module Two

- **Entering/Editing Data**
- **Deleting Information**
- **Adjusting Column Widths**
- **Creating Formulas**
- **Filling Data & Formulas**
- **Saving a Workbook**
- **Previewing/Printing**
- **Changing Page Setup**
- **Closing a File**

ENTERING INFORMATION

USAGE:

Excel allows you to type in words, numbers or formulas.

Click or tap in the cell you want to store the data in and then simply begin typing the word(s), number or formula.

If you make a mistake and want to start over, press [ESC].

Notice as you type, the entry is displayed both in the cell and in the formula bar. A thin, blinking cursor appears to the right of the entry and moves as you type.

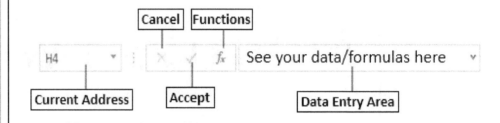

Instructor Note:

The formula bar needs to be understood – though students are not entering formulas at this point.

Simply discuss the purpose of each item on the Formula Bar.

If you make a mistake while typing, use the [←BACKSPACE] key to correct what has already been entered.

You cannot use the arrow keys at this time to make corrections! Pressing an arrow key at this point will enter what you have typed in the cell and then automatically move the pointer in the direction of the arrow key you pressed.

Two symbols also pop up to the left of the formula bar. The ✓ can be used by mouse users instead of pressing the [ENTER] key. The ✗ is used like the [ESC] key to cancel.

When entering text, words are automatically left aligned within the cell while numbers are placed to the right.

While entering columns of numbers, the column heading may not align correctly with the values. If text is wider than the cell it is stored in, it will appear to "spill" into the adjacent cell(s), providing they are empty.

THE AUTOCOMPLETE FEATURE

To save you from typing the same entry more than once, Excel offers a feature referred to as **AutoComplete**.

This feature tries to predict (based on your previous entries), what word you are currently entering. For example, if you have entered the word **East** in one or more cells in the current column, the next time you begin a cell entry with the letter **E**, Excel will fill the cell with the word **East**.

To accept this entry, simply press `ENTER`. Naturally, Excel is not always correct so if the prediction is wrong, simply continue typing.

PICK FROM LIST

If you are working in a very large workbook within a column of repeated entries, instead of continuously having to type the entries in yourself, you can select them from a list that Excel automatically generates from the current column entries.

Be sure that you are in a column filled with multiple entries before continuing.

Move to the cell where you want the entry placed. Click the **[RIGHT]** mouse button once or tap and hold (if using a touch screen device).

From the pop-up menu that appears, select **Pick from Drop-down List....**

Boston
Dallas
Denver
Irvine
Los Angeles

From the list provided, select the entry you would like placed in the current cell.

NOTE: For this feature to work, you must select a cell directly beneath the current list of entries. If a blank cell exists between the current entries and your selected cell, the list will be empty.

PRACTICE EXERCISE

Instructions:	❶	Type in the information as it appears below.
	❷	Do not worry about the information lining up at the moment. We will go back later and correct any problems.

CITY	JANUARY	FEBRUARY	MARCH
Chicago	4	4	6
Denver	4	6	6
Dallas	8	5	4
Boston	7	8	8
Los Angeles	12	15	22
New York	4	6	7

EDITING DATA

USAGE:

If you type something in a cell and then decide later to change or correct it, place your pointer on the cell to edit and reactivate it by selecting from one of the two methods mentioned below:

Double-Click or **Double-Tap** on the cell you want to edit.

If you prefer using the keyboard, press F2

Your cursor will appear within the cell in the form of a vertical bar and you will be able to use ←BACKSPACE and DEL to make corrections.

You can also use the following keys for movement while editing:

HOME	Moves to the beginning of the entry.
END	Moves to the end of the entry.
→	Moves the cursor to the right one character.
←	Moves the cursor to the left one character.
CTRL + →	Moves the cursor one word right.
CTRL + ←	Moves the cursor on word left.

When done editing the cell, press ENTER or click/tap on ✓ .

DELETING DATA

USAGE:

Although you can type over existing data (simply replacing it with the new information), there may be times when you would like to clear a cell out so that nothing is stored in it. In those instances, it would make sense to delete the contents of the selected cell(s).

To delete the contents of a cell, follow these steps:

❶   While pointing to the cell you want to clear, click the **[RIGHT]** mouse button or tap and hold (if using a touch screen).

❷

✂ Cut
⧉ Copy
⧉ **Paste Options:**
⧉
Paste Special...
↻ Smart Lookup
Insert...
Delete...
Clear Contents
Quick Analysis
Filter ▶
Sort ▶
New Comment
New Note
Format Cells...
Pick From Drop-down List...
Define Name...
Link ▶

From the pop-up menu that appears, select **Clear Contents**.

If you prefer using the keyboard to delete the contents of a cell:

Move to the cell and press the [DEL] key once.

Instructor Note:

Explain the difference between these options and why you'd want to use each.

For example, clearing contents doesn't clear the formatting so the next time you enter something in that cell, it'll take on the formatting previously applied.

CLEARING A CELL

Excel not only allows you to clear the contents of a cell (the actual data), but also the format and/or comments attached to the cell.

A single cell may contain one or more of the following:

Formats   Includes fonts, bold, borders surrounding the cell(s), as well as, number formats (e.g., dollar signs).

Contents   The data stored within the cell (numbers or text).

Comments   Can be attached to a cell to explain the reasoning behind its entry (e.g., when entering complex formulas). These comments are usually not printed.

Hyperlinks   Includes any hyperlinks that have been attached to the current cell.

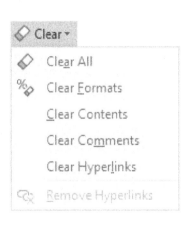

Click or tap this tool (located within the "Editing" section on the Home Ribbon).

Choose what you want to clear from the pull-down list provided.

OOPS! UNDOING THE DELETION

Excel has the capability of remembering the last several actions performed and allows you to change your mind about most changes you have made.

Click or tap this tool (located towards the top left corner of your screen) to undo the last action.

| Bold |
| Typing '21' in G4 |
| Typing 'This' in E1 |
| Typing 'Irvine' in E7 |
| Typing 'Los Angeles' in E6 |
| Typing 'Denver' in E5 |
| Typing 'Dallas' in E4 |
| Typing 'Boston' in E3 |
| Typing '+b2' in B1 |
| Normal View |
| Page Break Preview |
| Page Layout View |
| Cancel |

If you click or tap on the down arrow ☑ (to the right of the tool), you can scroll through the last several actions.

Move your mouse down the list to highlight the number of actions to undo. They must be done in sequence!

REDOING COMMANDS

If you undo a set of actions and then change your mind (again), you can always "Redo" what you have just undone.

Click or tap on this tool (located towards the top left corner of your screen) to redo the last undo.

WORKING WITH BLOCKS

USAGE:

Many commands and operations require that you work on more than one cell at a time. While you may not require the entire worksheet, you may need to work on a **Block** of cells.

A block includes any group of cells in a rectangular format, as shown in the illustration below.

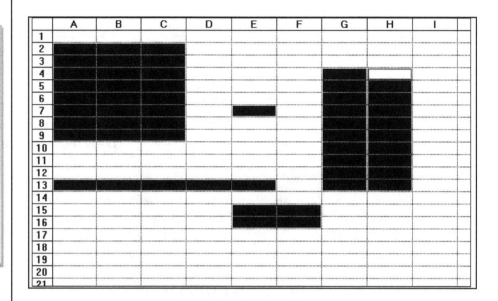

Every block of cells has a beginning and ending address. The beginning address is the address of the cell in the top-left corner of the block whereas the ending address is the cell in the lower-right.

Normally, in the English language we use a dash to indicate a block of numbers, as in pages 5-20. Excel, however, requires that you use the colon between the beginning and ending addresses. Remember that the dash represents subtraction in spreadsheet programs. For example, the block C3:E14 refers to cells C3 through E14.

There are many commands (e.g., deleting, copying, formatting) that require the use of blocks.

MOUSE SHAPES

When working with Excel, it is very important to keep an eye on the mouse pointer as it changes shape depending on its current function, as discussed below:

 If the mouse is in the shape of a thick cross, it can be used to select a single cell or block of cells for editing purposes.

The mouse changes to the thick cross when placed in the middle of a cell. Dragging the pointer when it is this shape simply highlights cells.

 If the mouse is in the shape of a diagonal arrow with a four-way crosshair attached to it, you can move the contents of the currently selected cell or block of cells to another location within the worksheet.

The mouse changes to this only when the tip of the arrow points to one of the outer borders of the selected cell block or when pointing to a graphic item. Dragging the pointer when it is in this shape actually picks up the contents of the cell(s) and moves them to another location.

+ If the mouse is in the shape of a thin cross-hair, you can fill a formula or other information into adjacent cells within the worksheet.

The mouse pointer changes to a thin cross-hair only when the tip of the arrow is placed in the small square located in the bottom right-corner of a cell. Dragging the pointer when it is in this shape fills data.

Instructor Note:

Make sure students can see each of these mouse shapes so they understand what happens when they click – depending on which shape is displayed.

SELECTING A BLOCK OF CELLS

Move to the middle of the first cell. Mouse users will see the pointer change to a thick cross-hair. Click or tap and begin dragging to highlight the cells.

To select an entire column or row, click or tap on the letter of the column or the number of the row.

Hold the `SHIFT` key down and press the arrows to select a block.

SELECTING A CONTIGUOUS BLOCK OF CELLS

❶   Click or tap in the first cell of the block to be highlighted.

❷   Move to the last cell (do <u>not</u> click or tap).

❸   In the last cell, hold the `SHIFT` key down and click or tap.

SELECTING NONCONTIGUOUS BLOCKS OF CELLS

❶   Click or tap on the first cell.

❷   Move to each cell or group of cells to be selected and hold `CTRL` down while you click or tap.

SELECTING THE ENTIRE WORKSHEET

Click Here	A	B
1		
2		

To select the entire worksheet, point to the square - just above the first row indicator and to the left of the first column indicator and click or tap. The entire worksheet will be highlighted.

ADJUSTING COLUMN WIDTH & ROW HEIGHT

USAGE:

Sometimes cell entries are too long to fit into the standard width columns. Text will appear to "spill" over into adjacent cells as long as those cells are empty. If the adjacent cells are not empty, Excel will truncate the text.

When entering large numbers, however, Excel will display the number in scientific notation if the column is not wide enough to display the entire number. However, if you apply formatting (such as dollar signs), Excel will automatically adjust the column to fit the largest entry so that the number remains visible.

Should a cell be too narrow for text or numbers that you have entered, you can widen the column in which the entry is located by following the steps outlined below:

Instructor Note:

Resizing columns and rows is done all the time in Excel so be sure students have time to practice.

❶ Point to the column heading area to the right of the lettered column to adjust. Mouse users will see the pointer change to a cross-hair ✛ indicating you are on the margin line.

❷ Click or tap and drag the column margin line either to the right (expanding it) or to the left (shrinking it).

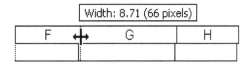

In the example above, column F is being stretched to the right. Notice the "cross-hair".

NOTE:	To change the height of a row, point to the bottom line of the row number (located on the left side of the worksheet). Mouse users will see a thin cross-hair appear. Drag up/down to adjust the row's height.

TIP:	If you **double-click** or **double-tap** the column or row margin line, Excel will automatically adjust the width of the column or row to fit the largest cell in the column/row.

NOTE:	You may also change the width of multiple columns or rows at once, by selecting the columns or rows (by dragging over each of the column letters or row numbers to select them) before adjusting their width/height.

ENTERING A FORMULA

USAGE:

Formulas are used to obtain answers based on mathematical equations that you design. Formulas can be as simple as "2+2" or as complex as calculating the depreciation of fixed assets. When creating formulas, you may use actual values, cell addresses or a combination of the two.

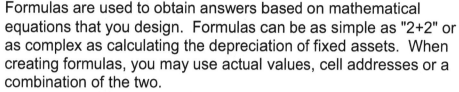

❶ The equal sign (=) is used to indicate to Excel that you are about to enter a formula. This also ensures that formulas beginning with a cell address are not mistaken for text.

❷ Next, you must enter the actual formula for Excel to calculate. When entering these formulas, the following basic mathematical operators are used:

+ (add)   - (subtract)   * (multiply)   / (divide)

❸ When a formula is complete and the ENTER key has been pressed, the result will be displayed in the current cell. The formula itself is displayed in the formula bar (located in the upper-left of the screen next to the cell address).

NOTE:	*In order to view a formula, you must select the cell in which it is stored.*

TIP:	*If you select a group of cells and look at the status bar (at bottom of the screen), Excel will display the total (sum) of the selected cells.*

USING CELL ADDRESSES

Excel has the ability to use a 'cell address' in place of an actual value when creating formulas. This means that you can type in a formula using cell addresses associated with the data instead of the actual numbers.

This can be extremely helpful if the values change on a regular basis since you wouldn't have to change the formula(s) every time the value changes.

By using a cell address in a formula, you are instructing Excel to get the current value stored at that address location for use in the formula.

For example, in the image below, you would refer to the 1st Qtr sales of Computers as B2 in your formulas instead of the value 300.

⊿	A	B	C	D	E	F
1		1st Qtr	2nd Qtr	3rd Qtr	4th Qtr	Total
2	Computers	$ 300	$ 548	$ 474	$ 684	$ 2,006
3	Printers	$ 450	$ 745	$ 523	$ 621	$ 2,339
4	Monitors	$ 657	$ 954	$ 748	$ 887	$ 3,246
5	Accessories	$ 485	$ 547	$ 316	$ 592	$ 1,940

Using the example shown above, to create a formula that calculates the total sales for Computers, you would move to cell F2 and enter the following formula:

=B2+C2+D2+E2

This provides you the flexibility of changing the cell values and having the totals immediately recalculated without changing the formula itself.

To create a total for the entire 1st Qtr, you would move to cell B6 and enter the following formula:

=B2+B3+B4+B5

CORRECTING FORMULAS

Excel can help to locate errors by checking your formulas for common mistakes and offering a suggested correction.

When you press the ENTER key after typing in a formula, Excel checks the formula for possible syntax errors.

If an error is encountered, a dialog box will pop-up explaining what Excel thinks is the problem with the formula and asking if it should correct the formula based on its suggestion.

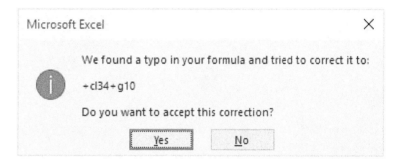

PRACTICE EXERCISE

Instructions:	❶	Widen columns B and C so that there is plenty of room for the column headings.
	❷	Add the heading to column E.
	❸	Enter a formula to calculate the quarter total by adding the three months together.
		Enter the formula in cell **E2** only! The next exercise will teach you how to fill the formula to the other cells in column E.

Instructor Note:

We use two exercises all day for the class so if you don't use this one, be sure to provide your own at this point.

CITY	JANUARY	FEBRUARY	MARCH	QUARTER TOTAL
Chicago	4	4	6	14
Denver	4	6	6	
Dallas	8	5	4	
Boston	7	8	8	
Los Angeles	12	15	22	
New York	4	6	7	

USING THE AUTO FILL

USAGE:

Instructor Note:

AutoFill is a terrific feature yet students often select it without meaning to (not paying attention to the shape of their mouse when dragging). Be sure to cover this feature in detail.

Excel offers a quick way to fill formulas from one cell to many within the worksheet. This command instructs Excel to copy cells from one row/column in a selection to adjacent cells of the selection.

❶ Move to the small square in the lower right corner of the cell containing the formula you want to copy. Mouse users should see the pointer change to a thin crosshair ✛.

❷ Click or tap and drag so that all destination cells are selected. When you let go of the mouse or your finger (if using a touch screen), the formula will be "filled" in all cells.

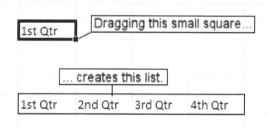

Filling also works for text and numbers without formulas, such as months or quarters (shown in the example above).

Excel's auto fill feature will fill a block of cells with either numbers or text depending on what is located in the first cell.

As you begin filling the destination cells with months, Excel will display the name of each month as it is being filled so that you know how far to fill.

TIP:	To quickly fill the current cell with the contents of the cell above it, press **CTRL**+**D** (to fill downward).
	To fill the current cell with the contents of the cell to the left of it, press **CTRL**+**R** (to fill right).

When working with numbers, however, you must enter two cells of data so that Excel knows what increments the numbers should be increased by each time. If you only enter a single number and then try to create a fill based on that single cell, Excel will simply copy the number down the worksheet.

To fill cells with a series of numbers, follow these steps:

❶ Select the two cells containing the numbers. Once the two cells have been selected, release the mouse button.

❷ Move to the bottom right corner of the second cell. Mouse users should see the pointer change to a thin cross-hair ✛.

❸ Click or tap and then drag to fill the other cells.

USING THE FILL TOOL

You can fill cells in any direction and into any range of adjacent cells using the fill tool.

⬇ Fill ▾   After selecting the cells to fill, click or tap on this tool (within the Editing section on the Home Ribbon).

A pull-down list of fill options will be displayed:

⬇	Down
➡	Right
⬆	Up
⬅	Left
	Across Worksheets...
	Series...
	Justify
▦	Flash Fill

Select the direction of the fill or define the series to use when filling.

AUTO FILL OPTIONS

Once you have used the auto fill feature, a small icon 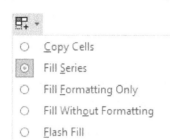 will be placed in the bottom right corner of the last filled cell.

When you click or tap this icon, a list of auto fill options is displayed. **Copy Cells** instructs Excel to copy the data and formatting from the original cell to the destination cells.

The **Fill Formatting Only** option is used to copy the format from the original cell to the destination cells. This does not copy the data from the original cell.

Select **Fill Without Formatting** to copy the data from the original cell to the destination cells without changing the existing format.

NOTE:	*These auto fill options will vary depending on what you have just filled (e.g., a formula, a number, a month).*

USING FLASH FILL

The **Flash Fill** feature recognizes patterns in the data as you enter it. For example, if you enter both first and last names in a column and then begin entering first names in the next column, the Flash Fill feature will recognize that the first names correspond with the names in the other column and offer to fill the data for you.

Type the first two entries in order for Excel to recognize the pattern. As you begin the second item, Excel should recognize the pattern and will offer to fill the remaining cells (as shown in the example along the left).

If the suggestion is correct, press `ENTER` to accept the flash fill.

Once you have used Flash Fill, a new icon will appear beside the column, with options for undoing the fill, accepting the fill or selecting the blank/changed cells.

Instructor Note:

This is a really useful feature so be sure to explain it carefully and allow students time to practice a bit on their own.

SPELL CHECKING THE WORKSHEET

USAGE:

Instructor Note:

Even though it's not as obvious, explain that it's important to always spell check workbooks to ensure no typos are included.

Before saving and printing the worksheet out for others to read, you should always check it for typing errors. By comparing words in your file against the dictionary, Excel can check your spelling and alert you of possible mistakes.

For each word that the program cannot find in its dictionary, Excel asks you what to do. You can choose to change the spelling of the word, suggest alternatives, leave the word as it was entered, or add the word to the dictionary. Excel also checks for repeated words and incorrect capitalization.

Spelling

Click or tap the **Spelling** tool (located within the "Proofing" section on the Review Ribbon).

Excel will display the following box:

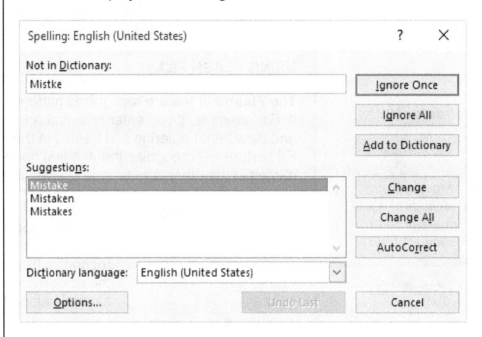

The top section of the box contains the first unrecognized word. The lower portion of the dialog box contains suggestions for correcting the flagged word.

The following buttons are provided within the spell-checking box:

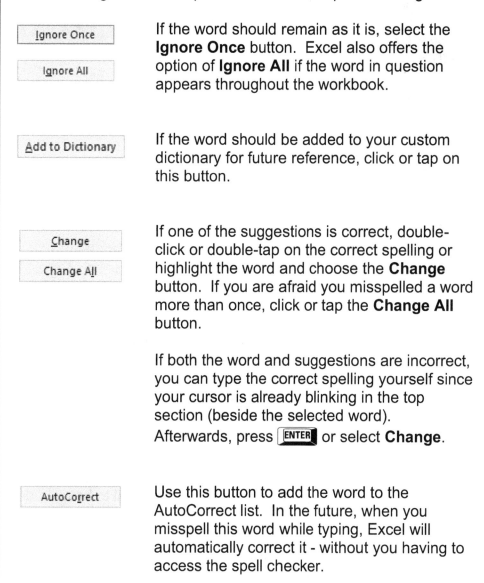

Ignore Once / Ignore All	If the word should remain as it is, select the **Ignore Once** button. Excel also offers the option of **Ignore All** if the word in question appears throughout the workbook.
Add to Dictionary	If the word should be added to your custom dictionary for future reference, click or tap on this button.
Change / Change All	If one of the suggestions is correct, double-click or double-tap on the correct spelling or highlight the word and choose the **Change** button. If you are afraid you misspelled a word more than once, click or tap the **Change All** button.
	If both the word and suggestions are incorrect, you can type the correct spelling yourself since your cursor is already blinking in the top section (beside the selected word). Afterwards, press ENTER or select **Change**.
AutoCorrect	Use this button to add the word to the AutoCorrect list. In the future, when you misspell this word while typing, Excel will automatically correct it - without you having to access the spell checker.
Undo Last	Reverses the latest action made during the current spell-checking session.

This button is used to change the options associated with spelling features.

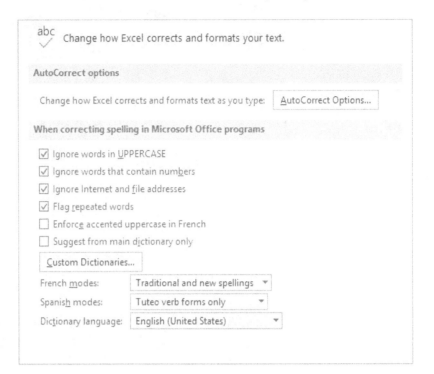

You will be taken to a box that provides a variety of options to customize how the spell checker works. For example, you can choose to ignore words in uppercase, ignore words that contain numbers, ignore Internet and file addresses, specify whether to flag repeated words, enforce accented uppercase in French, suggest from the main dictionary only, or select custom dictionaries to use.

Click or tap Custom Dictionaries... to add or modify custom dictionaries, such as medical and legal to be used during spell checking.

Once all options are selected, choose OK . You will be returned to the original spell-checking box where you can continue.

After running the spell checker, save your workbook with all the corrections.

SAVING YOUR WORKBOOK

USAGE:

After having entered data in your workbook, you will want to save it and assign a name that will allow you to easily find it again. If you open the File Tab on the ribbon, you will notice two options for saving a workbook: **Save** and **Save As**.

Save is the normal save feature which will ask you the first time you save a file to assign a name to it. From that point on, choosing SAVE will simply update the file to include the new information. On the other hand, **Save As** saves an existing file under a new name or as a different format to be imported into another program.

 Click or tap the **Save** icon (on the Quick Access Bar).

When you first save a workbook, you will need to specify where you want to save it:

 Recent — Use this to save the workbook in a folder that has been recently used.

 OneDrive

 OneDrive - Personal he@va.com — Use this to store the file in your Microsoft OneDrive account instead of your local computer. This allows you to access the file from anywhere. If you are already logged in, you'll see the bottom option.

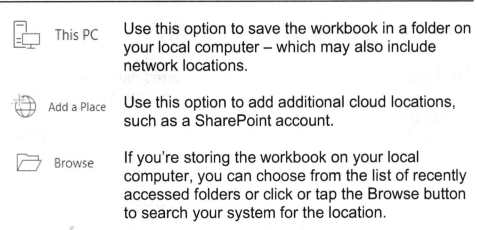

| | This PC | Use this option to save the workbook in a folder on your local computer – which may also include network locations. |

| | Add a Place | Use this option to add additional cloud locations, such as a SharePoint account. |

| | Browse | If you're storing the workbook on your local computer, you can choose from the list of recently accessed folders or click or tap the Browse button to search your system for the location. |

Once you select a storage location, you will be taken to the dialog box that will prompt you to enter a file name, as shown below:

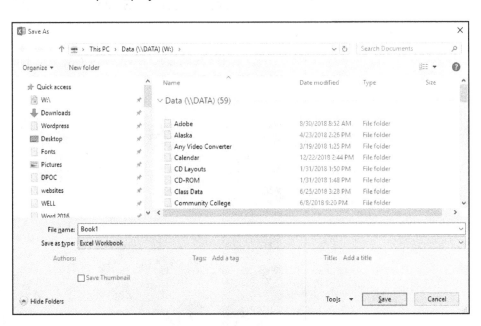

Along the left side of the dialog box, Excel displays the **Navigation Pane**. This pane lists common/favorite locations (links) as well as a section for browsing your folders and drives.

You can hide/display the "Folders List" section at the bottom of this area by clicking or tapping on the ∨ ∧ arrows.

Use the address bar to determine the path, as shown below:

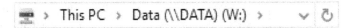

Notice the path is displayed horizontally on the bar. For example, in the diagram shown above the currently selected item is the "Data" drive (W) which is available on your computer. To get to that folder, you had to first go to "This PC", then the Data drive (W).

This layout is commonly referred to as "bread crumbs" because it shows you the path that was taken to get to the current location.

You can easily move to another folder on the "W" drive by clicking or tapping on the ⟩ arrow beside the drive name and then selecting a different folder to view.

In the box provided, enter a name for the new file. Letters, numbers and spaces are allowed. Enter 1-255 characters.

Notice that Excel defaults to assigning the "xlsx" extension.

If you want to save the workbook in another format (such as another spreadsheet application or any previous version of Excel so that someone else can edit the workbook who does not have this version), click on the down arrow ⌄ beside the box labeled **Save as type** and select the format from the list provided.

Enter a name for the workbook in the box labeled **File name** and then click or tap on ⎣ Save ⎦ to actually save the workbook.

> **TIP:** The shortcut key (from within the workbook) for saving is ⟦CTRL⟧ + ⟦S⟧.

Instructor Note:

If you had students create the sample in the manual, have them name this workbook CITIES.

PRINTING

USAGE:

Obviously, you'll need to print at some point. You can choose what part of the workbook to print (such as the current page, multiple pages or the entire file). In addition, you can specify which printer to use and how many copies you'd like.

Click or tap on the **File** tab on the Ribbon and select **Print** from the pull-down list of options.

The Print window will be displayed:

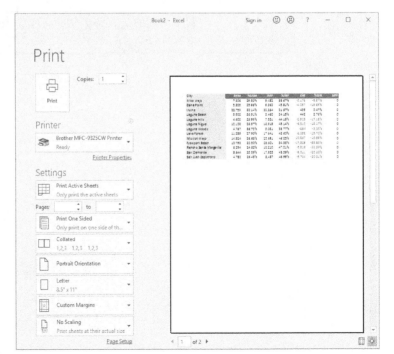

A preview of the workbook as it will be printed appears along the right side of this window.

◁ | 1 | of 4 ▷   Moves between pages while previewing (along the right side of the window).

Options along the left side of the window include:

| Brother MFC-9325CW Ready | Click or tap this button to select the printer you want to use. |

Printer Properties   Click or tap this item to access additional properties for the printout.

| Print Active Sheets Only print the active sheets |
| Pages: [ ] to [ ] |

Use this section to specify exactly what portion of the workbook should be printed.

| Print One Sided Only print on one side of th... | Choose whether you are printing single or double-sided. |

| Collated 1,2,3 1,2,3 1,2,3 | You can choose to collate multi-page workbooks so you don't have to go back and arrange them manually. |

| Portrait Orientation | Choose whether you are printing landscape or portrait. |

| Letter 8.5" x 11" | Use this section to specify your paper size. |

| Normal Margins Left: 0.7" Right: 0.7" | Set your margins for the printout. |

| No Scaling Print sheets at their actual size | If you're printing a large workbook and want to condense the printing, you can scale it to print multiple pages per sheet of paper. |

Page Setup   Provides detailed document settings.

Copies: [1]   Allows you to specify the number of copies.

| Print | Click or tap this button to begin printing. |

TIP: *The shortcut key for printing is* `CTRL` + `P`.

CHANGING THE PAGE SETUP

USAGE:

Before you actually print a worksheet, you may want to customize the file to change margins, adjust page orientation, add headers/footers, or modify other features.

CHANGING MARGINS

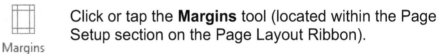

Margins

Click or tap the **Margins** tool (located within the Page Setup section on the Page Layout Ribbon).

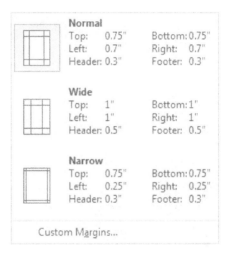

Select the new margin setting from the list provided.

If you need a margin setting that is not included in this pull-down list, click or tap on **Customize Margins….** (located at the bottom of the list) to open a dialog box where you can enter custom margins.

CHANGING ORIENTATION

Click or tap the **Orientation** tool (located within the Page Setup section on the Page Layout Ribbon).

Select the page orientation from the two diagrams provided.

CHANGING PAPER SIZE

Click or tap the **Size** tool (located within the Page Setup section on the Page Layout Ribbon).

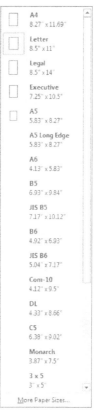

Select the paper size you would like to use when printing your worksheet. If you don't see a size in the list, click on **More Paper Sizes…** to access the Page Setup dialog box.

CHANGING THE PRINT AREA

Print
Area ▾

If you want to print a specific area of the worksheet, select the blocks of cells to be printed and then click or tap the **Print Area** tool (located within the Page Setup section on the Page Layout Ribbon) to define or clear the print area.

Choose to either set the print area or clear it.

SETTING/REMOVING PAGE BREAKS

Breaks
▾

To force a new page to start at a specific row and column location, select the cell within the column and row where the new page should begin and then click or tap the **Breaks** tool (located within the Page Setup section on the Page Layout Ribbon). The current row and column will each begin on a new page. Be sure to print preview before printing.

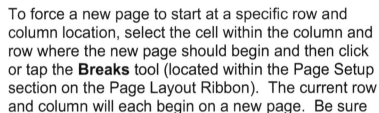

Choose whether you want to insert a page break at the current location, remove one, or reset all page breaks within the worksheet.

APPLYING A GRAPHICS BACKGROUND

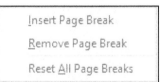

Background

Click or tap on the **Background** tool (located within the Page Setup section on the Page Layout Ribbon) to insert a graphic file as a background for your document. You'll be taken to a dialog box where you can search your system for a picture or texture file.

DEFINING PRINT TITLES

Print
Titles

Click or tap the **Print Titles** tool (located within the Page Setup section on the Page Layout Ribbon) to specify which rows and columns are to be repeated on each page. You will be taken to a dialog box where you can define which columns/rows to repeat.

SCALING THE DOCUMENT

Use these tools (located within the **Scale to Fit** section on the Page Layout Ribbon) to specify an exact size for the worksheet when printing.

SHEET OPTIONS

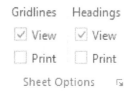

Use these checkboxes (located within the **Sheet Options** section on the Page Layout Ribbon) to specify whether gridlines and column/row headings will be displayed on the screen and/or included in your printout.

ACCESSING THE PAGE SETUP DIALOG BOX

Click or tap on the **Page Setup Dialog Box Launcher** (located on the Page Layout Ribbon).

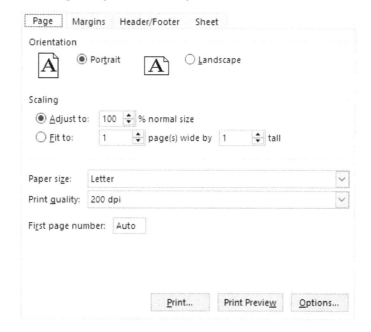

Within the tab labeled **Page**, the following options are available:

Orientation	Use this section to change the paper orientation to **Landscape** or **Portrait**.
Scaling	This section allows you to enlarge or reduce the printout. Not all printers will be able to use this feature.
	Use the **Adjust to:** option to reduce or enlarge the output from 10 to 400 percent of the original size.
	Use the **Fit to:** option to specify exactly how many pages wide or tall you want the final printout to be.
Paper size	Provides various paper sizes to choose from. Available sizes will vary from printer to printer.
Print quality	Allows you to specify the resolution (dots per inch) for printing. The higher the number, the better the quality - but it also takes longer.
First page number	Leave this option at **Auto** to start page numbering at the next sequential number or enter a number with which the first page should begin.

CUSTOMIZING MARGINS

To change the margins, click on the **Margins** tab, as shown below:

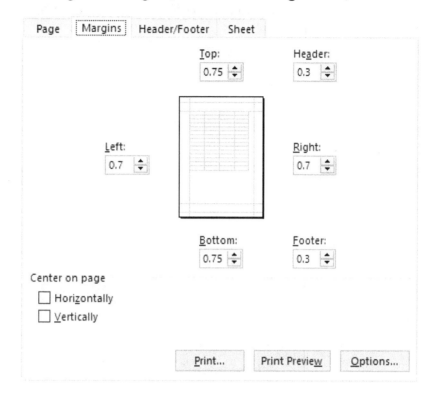

Top/Bottom	Use this section to change the top and bottom distance between the edge of the paper and the printout. Be sure to leave enough room for your header/footer.
Left/Right	Use this section to change the left and right distances between the edge of the paper and the printout.
Header/Footer	Use this section to change the top and bottom distances between the edge of the paper and the header and/or footer. Make sure that this value is smaller than the **Top/Bottom** margins or the header will overlap the data.
Center on page	This option is used to balance a printout by centering pages **Horizontally** (between the left and right margins) and/or **Vertically** (between the top and bottom margins).

CUSTOMIZING HEADERS/FOOTERS

To customize or remove the headers/footers, click on the tab labeled **Header/Footer**, as shown below:

Page	Margins	Header/Footer	Sheet

Header:
(none) ⌄

Custom Header...   Custom Footer...

Footer:
(none) ⌄

☐ Different odd and even pages
☐ Different first page
☑ Scale with document
☑ Align with page margins

Print...   Print Preview   Options...

The top section is a sample of what the current header will display.

In the section called **Header** is a pull-down list of predefined headers. Click or tap on the down arrow ⌄ and choose from the list of available headers.

In the section called **Footer** is a pull-down list of predefined footers.

Click or tap on the down arrow ⌄ and choose from the list of available footers.

Notice the checkboxes along the bottom of this box which allow you to choose different odd and even page headers/footers, a different first page header/footer, scale the header/footer to match the document, and align the header/footer with the page margins.

Instructor Note:

Allow students time to insert a header in their worksheet.

To customize the header/footer click or tap one of these buttons:

The custom header and footer dialog boxes look the same:

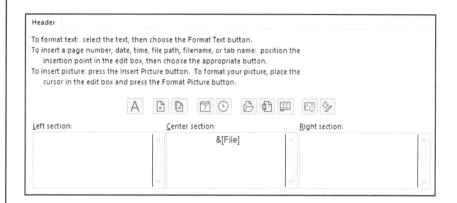

Use the **Left**, **Center** and **Right** sections of the box to enter text. The section you type it in will determine where the header/footer text will be placed on the printed page.

Use the following buttons to add special options:

A	Allows you to customize the font.
	Inserts the current **Page Number**.
	Adds the **Total number of pages** in the printout.
	Adds the **Date** to the header/footer.
	Adds the **Time** to the header/footer.
	Adds the **Path & Filename** to the header/footer.
	Adds the **Filename** to the header/footer.
	Adds the **Tab Name** to the header/footer.
	Allows you to insert a **Picture** in the header/footer.
	If you have a picture, use this to **Format the Picture**.

SHEET PRINTOUT OPTIONS

Click on the **Sheet** tab to customize the print features that affect the overall sheet, as shown below:

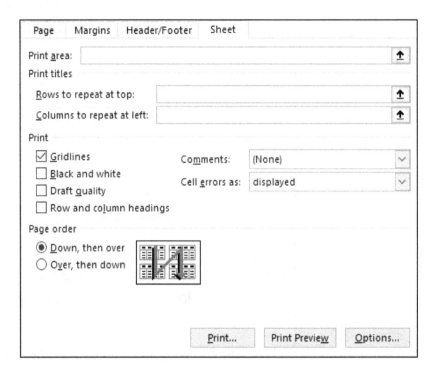

Print area	Use this section to specify the block to be printed. If you selected a block before you entered this box, the block will already be displayed. If not, you may enter the range as **A1:B15** to specify that the block from A1 to B15 should be printed. You can enter more than one range if you separate the ranges with a comma - as in **A1:B15,D20:F40**.
Print titles	This section allows you to specify rows to be printed along the top or the columns to be printed along the left of each page. To specify a range, click in the row or column section and then type the block.
	Click or tap this button (to the right of these two sections) to return to the worksheet to select the block. When done, reactivate the Page Setup box.

Print   You can choose to either display **Gridlines** or
                          suppress the sheet gridlines from printing.

                          Black and white is used to print in black and white
                          for faster printing.

                          Checking the **Draft quality** option speeds up the
                          printout by printing less graphics and suppresses
                          the gridlines.

                          Check the **Row and column headings** box to print
                          the row numbers and column letters around the
                          border of the printout.

                          Depending on your preference, you can choose to
                          print **Comments** on a separate page at the end of
                          your document or as they are displayed in the
                          worksheet.

                          You can also choose how **Cell errors** will be printed
                          (blank, as they appear in the cell or with the #N/A
                          indicator).

Page order   If your printout will be several pages wide, use this
                          section to specify the order pages are to be printed.
                          You can choose to print **Down, then Across** or
                          Across, then Down.

You should notice the ⌈ Options... ⌉ button to the right side of each of
the tabbed boxes. This button is used to access the "Printer
Properties" dialog box.

You should also notice the ⌈ Print Preview ⌉ button within each of the
tabbed dialog boxes. If you want to see how the worksheet will
print based on the current settings, click on this button.

Once you have made your selections from the various tabs, click or
tap the ⌈ OK ⌉ button to save your settings.

CLOSING A DOCUMENT

USAGE:

Although you can have several windows (workbooks) open at the same time, it is usually a good idea to close a file once you have saved and printed it if you no longer need to continue editing.

 Click or tap on the close button in the upper right corner of the window to close the current workbook. If you only have one document open and you click on this icon, Excel will close the entire program.

If you only have one workbook open and don't want to close the entire application, you can close the workbook by accessing the **File** tab on the Ribbon, as shown below:

Select **Close** from the pull-down list of options.

NOTE:	If you have made changes to the workbook and have not saved those changes, Excel will ask whether you want to save the changes before closing the file.

CREATING A NEW WORKBOOK

USAGE:

When you first run Excel, you are taken into a blank, untitled workbook where you may begin entering data. If, however, you are in the midst of working with one file and then decide to create another workbook, you will need to instruct Excel as to what type of new document you want to create.

You can either create another blank workbook or base the new file on one of Excel's built-in templates or from one of your own existing templates. A template is used to determine the basic structure of the workbook and can contain predefined settings, such as formulas, formatting, and macros.

To create a new workbook, select **New** from the pull-down list of options within the File tab on the Ribbon.

The following window will be displayed:

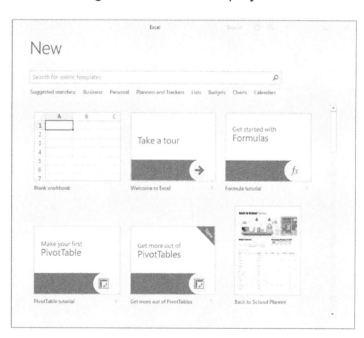

Instructor Note:

Templates are discussed in the final module of this manual so don't go into detail here.

Do explain that every new workbook is based on a template and that the default one is labeled "Blank workbook".

When you click on one of the templates, a pop-up window is displayed with a preview of the template and a short description.

If there are templates that you'll be using on a regular basis, you may want to pin them to the list so that they remain at the top for easy access.

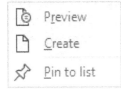

To quickly pin a template, point to the template and then click or tap on (located along the top right corner of its preview) or click your [RIGHT] mouse button once and choose **Pin to list** from the pop-up menu.

If you change your mind, click or tap on the icon (located on the template preview) to unpin the template.

To actually use one of the templates, click on the one you want to use. A pop-up window is displayed with a preview of the template, a short description, and its size:

Click or tap this button to create a new workbook based on the selected template.

The new workbook will be created - based on the template you have selected.

NOTE: *To quickly create a new blank workbook without first having to access the menu, press* `CTRL`+`N`.

SWITCHING BETWEEN MULTIPLE WORKBOOKS

When working with two or more open workbooks, you can switch between them by accessing the **View** ribbon and then clicking on the tool labeled **Switch Windows.**

Alternatively, you can quickly switch between open workbooks using the Windows taskbar (located along the bottom of your screen):

Either point or click on the icon to display a preview of each of your opened workbooks, as shown below:

X DSCC Membership List.xlsx - Ex...	X DFOC Membership List.xlsx - Ex...	X Newport Beach CCO list.xlsx - E...

X Excel

Next, simply click the workbook you wish to work with.

PRACTICE EXERCISE

Instructions:	❶	Create a new file based on the following information.
	❷	Create a formula in cell E2 to calculate the quarterly totals.
	❸	Copy the formula down to the other cells in column E. Your totals should match the ones shown below.
	❹	When you are done, save (name it **REGIONS**) and print the file before closing it.

REGION	OCT	NOV	DEC	QTR. TOTAL
Pacific	2.3	1.8	1.2	5.3
Northwest	1.6	1.1	.9	3.6
Northeast	2.5	2.2	2	6.7
Gulf	3.1	2.9	2.5	8.5
Southeast	2.6	2.1	1.8	6.5

Module Three

- Opening a Workbook
- Moving Data
- Alignment
- Formatting Values
- Inserting/Deleting

OPENING AN EXISTING WORKBOOK

USAGE:

If you want to work on an existing file, you must open it.

Choosing to open a file will place the requested workbook in another window so that more than one file can be open at the same time.

You can then switch between the opened workbooks using the taskbar across the bottom of your screen or by accessing the View Ribbon.

To open workbook stored on your computer, select **Open** from the pull-down list of options within the File tab on the Ribbon.

The following window will be displayed:

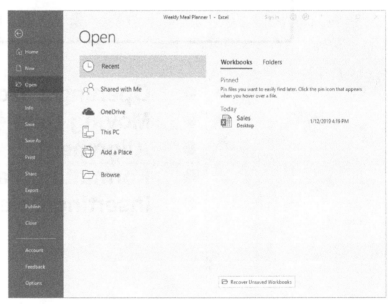

Notice your most recently accessed files are listed along the right.

Your first step is to select where the file is stored:

🕐	Recent	This is the default option. Excel automatically displays files you have recently been working on so that you can quickly return to them.
⧉	Shared with Me	If you are signed in to your Microsoft account, you can use this option to access files that have been shared with you.
☁	OneDrive	Use this if you want to open a workbook that has been stored on the Internet rather than a local computer.
🖥	This PC	Use this option to open a file that was stored in a folder on your local computer – which may also include network locations.
🌐	Add a Place	Use this to add a new OneDrive or SharePoint location from which to open files.

> **TIP:**   *If there are files or folders that you access often, you can "**pin**" them to the list so that they are always available, whenever you access the Open dialog box.*
>
> *To pin a file/folder, point to it (from within the list) and then click or tap on the 📌 icon.*
>
> *If you change your mind and no longer need the document/folder pinned to the list, point to the item and then click or tap on 📌 to remove it.*

📂	Browse	If you're opening a workbook that was stored on your local computer, you can choose from the list of recently accessed folders or click or tap on the Browse button to search your system for the folder storing the file.

Once you specify where the workbook is located, the following dialog box will be displayed:

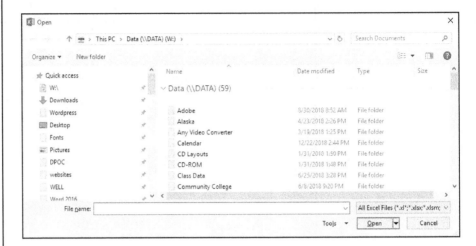

Along the left side of the dialog box, Excel displays the **Navigation Pane**. This pane lists common/favorite locations (links) as well as a section for browsing your folders and drives.

The address bar is displayed, as shown below:

Notice that the path is displayed horizontally on the bar. For example, in the diagram shown above the currently selected location is the "Data" drive (W:) which is on your computer/network. To get to that folder, you had to first choose your computer, then the Data drive (W). You could then select the folder containing your Excel files.

This layout is commonly referred to as "bread crumbs" because it shows you the path that was taken to get to the current location.

In the example shown on the previous page, you can easily move to another folder on the "W" drive by clicking or tapping on beside the drive name and then selecting a different folder to view.

Across the top of the window are the following buttons:

Organize ▼   Click or tap this button to access the **Organize** pull-down menu. From the pull-down list, select the operation (e.g., cut, copy, paste, delete, rename) you want to perform on existing files listed within this box.

New folder   Click or tap this button to create a new folder.

When ready, double-click or double-tap on the name of the file to open or highlight the name and click or tap on [Open ▼] to open the file.

Instructor Note:

Discuss the various Open options and offer examples of each.

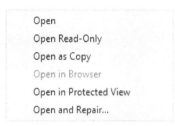

If you click or tap on the down arrow ⊡ beside the [Open ▼] button, you can choose from a list of options (such as opening the file as read-only or in your Web browser).

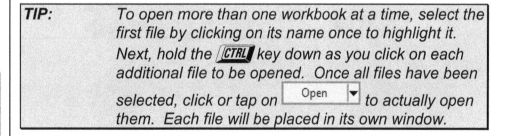

TIP: *To open more than one workbook at a time, select the first file by clicking on its name once to highlight it. Next, hold the CTRL key down as you click on each additional file to be opened. Once all files have been selected, click or tap on [Open ▼] to actually open them. Each file will be placed in its own window.*

Instructor Note:

Have students open the CITIES workbook.

TIP: *The shortcut key for opening files is CTRL + O.*

MOVING DATA

USAGE:

If you have created a workbook and then decide that a portion of the data should be placed in a different area within the file, you can move the contents of the cell(s) by cutting and pasting.

To move a single cell or block of cells from one location to another within your worksheet, follow these steps:

❶ Select the cell or block of cells to be moved.

❷ ✂ Cut   Click or tap on the **Cut** tool (which is located along the left portion of the Home Ribbon). Notice a marquee is placed around the selected cell(s).

❸ Move to the new location.

❹ Paste   Press ENTER or click/tap on the **Paste** tool.

> **Instructor Note:**
>
> *Point out the marquee that appears after cutting a cell or group of cells.*

TIP: *Using the keyboard, press CTRL+X to **Cut** and CTRL+V to **Paste**.*

COPYING TEXT

USAGE:

If you need a cell or block of cells copied to a new location, you can copy the cell(s). This leaves the information in its original location while taking a copy of it to the new location.

To copy a cell or block of cells from one location to another within the worksheet, follow these steps:

❶   Select the cell or block of cells to be copied.

❷      Click or tap on the **Copy** tool (which is located along the left side on the Home Ribbon). The block of cells is temporarily copied to the clipboard. Notice that a marquee is placed around the selected cell(s).

❸   Move to the new location.

❹   Press ENTER or click/tap on the **Paste** tool.

TIP: *Using the keyboard, press* CTRL+C *to Copy text and* CTRL+V *to Paste.*

PASTE FORMAT OPTIONS

Once an item has been pasted, a small clipboard icon  is displayed at that location within the workbook.

Click on this icon to select from a list of options that defines how the item should be pasted. These options depend on the type of content you are pasting, the application you are pasting from and the format of the text where you are pasting.

When you click or tap on the clipboard icon from within your workbook, a pull-down list appears offering several formatting options.

For example, you can choose to paste the item using either the original formatting codes or match it to the destination formatting codes. You can choose to paste the numbers or the formulas that the numbers are based on. You can also choose to insert an item as a graphic object that cannot be edited or as a hyperlink which can be used to link back to the item's original location.

You can also change the orientation of the copied data. For example, if you copied a row of data this will paste the data down a column instead of across a row.

Instructor Note:

These options are a bit overwhelming for a beginning class so you don't need to have them try each one out or even go into depth describing each option.

Go over the basics, such as pasting with the original format or choosing the destination format.

DRAGGING & DROPPING

USAGE:

Excel also allows you to cut/copy and paste data within a worksheet by using the **Drag & Drop** feature. This feature allows mouse users to "drag" the selected block to a new location. Once the location is reached, you simply "drop" the selected cells off.

MOVING CELLS WITH DRAG & DROP

To drag and drop a cell or block of cells, follow the steps below:

❶ Select the cell(s) to be moved.

❷ Point to one of the outer borders of the selected block.

Mouse users will see that the pointer changes to a four-way arrow .

❸ Begin dragging the block. An outline of the cells moves with you. Notice as you drag that Excel displays the current cell address so you are sure where you are dragging, as shown in the illustration below:

❹ When you reach the correct location, release the mouse button or your finger (if using a touch screen). The selection should have now been moved to the new location.

Instructor Note:

This is one of those things that users sometimes do by mistake so it's best to explain it early on so they understand what's happening when they see this.

COPYING CELLS WITH DRAG & DROP

To copy cells using drag and drop, follow the steps shown below:

❶ Select the cell(s) to be copied.

❷ Point to one of the outer borders of the selected block.

Mouse users will notice that the pointer changes to a four-way arrow .

❸ Hold the CTRL key down as you drag the block. An outline of the cells moves with you. The mouse pointer has a plus sign (+) attached to it. Notice as you drag the block that Excel displays the current cell address so you are sure where you are dragging, as shown in the illustration below:

D25

❹ When you reach the desired location, release the mouse button or your finger (if using a touch screen). The selected block should now have been copied to the new location.

MOVING DATA ACROSS SHEETS

If your workbook contains multiple sheets, you can also drag and drop cells from one sheet to another, as outlined in the steps shown below:

❶   Select the sheet and then the cell(s) to be moved.

❷   Point to one of the outer borders of the selected block.

Mouse users should notice that the pointer changes to a four-way arrow ⬩.

Instructor Note:

Even though they haven't worked with multiple worksheets (and don't in this class), show students how to drag across worksheets.

❸   Hold the ⟦ALT⟧ key down as you drag the block to the bottom of the screen (along the tabbed area listing the available sheets within the current file).

Continue holding down ⟦ALT⟧ as you drag the block to the tab representing the sheet you want to move the selected block of cells to.

An outline of the cells moves with you. Notice as you drag that Excel displays the current cell address so you are sure where you are dragging, as shown in the illustration below:

❹   When you reach the desired cell location within the new sheet, release the mouse button or your finger (if using a touch screen). The selected block should have now been moved to the new sheet location.

TIP:	The quickest way to move data between sheets is to use the keyboard. Select the cell(s) to be moved and press ⟦CTRL⟧+⟦X⟧. Move to the worksheet where the data should be pasted and press ⟦CTRL⟧+⟦V⟧.

COPYING DATA ACROSS SHEETS

You can also drag and drop cells to copy cells across sheets, as outlined in the steps below:

❶ Select the sheet and then the cell(s) to be copied.

❷ Point to one of the outer borders of the selected block.

Mouse users should notice that the pointer changes to a four-way arrow.

❸ Hold down both the CTRL and the ALT keys as you drag the block to the bottom of the screen (along the tabbed area listing the available sheets within the current file).

Continue holding down CTRL and ALT as you drag the block to the tab representing the sheet you want to copy the selected block of cells to.

An outline of the cells moves with you. Notice as you drag that Excel displays the current cell address so you are sure where you are dragging, as shown in the illustration below:

D25

❹ When you reach the desired cell location within the new sheet, release the mouse button or your finger (if using a touch screen). The selected block should have now been copied to the new sheet location.

> **TIP:** *The quickest way to copy data between sheets is to use the keyboard. Select the cell(s) to be copied and press* CTRL+C. *Move to the worksheet where the copied data should be pasted and press* CTRL+V.

WORKING WITH THE OFFICE CLIPBOARD

USAGE:

You can use the Office Clipboard to collect multiple items to be pasted within Excel or other Office applications. The standard Windows clipboard is only able to store one item at a time. You have to paste whatever you have cut or copied before your next cut/copy can be completed.

However, the Office Clipboard can store up to 24 items at a time, making it easy to collect multiple items to be pasted. If you copy a 25th item, the first item in your clipboard will automatically be removed to make room for the latest entry.

Depending on your computer's settings, choosing to copy an item and then copying a second one without pasting the first may trigger the Clipboard task pane to be displayed.

If the task pane is not automatically displayed, you can manually display it by accessing the following tool:

Click or tap on the **Clipboard Task Pane Launcher** ⌐⊾ (located along the far left side of the Home Ribbon).

The Office Clipboard will automatically be opened and placed within the left panel, as shown below:

The clipboard will display each of the cut or copied items - with the latest item placed at the top of the list. If you have cut or copied several entries, a scroll bar will be placed along the right side so that you can quickly move through the items.

A small icon is placed to the left of each object to indicate what application the cut or copied item was originally created in.

Move to the location to which the item(s) should be pasted.

Click or tap on the clipboard item to be pasted.

There are two tools available across the top of the clipboard:

| Paste All | Click or tap this tool to paste each of the items stored within the Office Clipboard in the current file (or within the current Office application). |

| Clear All | Click or tap this button to clear the contents of the Office Clipboard. It will also clear the Windows Clipboard. |

To remove a single item from the clipboard, point to the item you want to remove until you see a small down arrow ⊡.

Click or tap on the down arrow ⊡ and select **Delete** from the list of options.

CLIPBOARD OPTIONS

Towards the bottom of the clipboard is a button Options which is used to change the display settings for the Office Clipboard.

	Show Office Clipboard Automatically
	Show Office Clipboard When Ctrl+C Pressed Twice
	Collect Without Showing Office Clipboard
✓	Show Office Clipboard Icon on Taskbar
✓	Show Status Near Taskbar When Copying

From the five options available, check the box labeled **Show Office Clipboard Automatically** to open the clipboard within the task pane when two items in a row have been copied.

Select **Show Office Clipboard When Ctrl+C Pressed Twice** to display the Office Clipboard after pressing the copy shortcut keys.

Choose **Collect Without Showing Office Clipboard** if you prefer not to display the clipboard within the task pane when two items in a row have been copied. This option displays the clipboard icon on the taskbar even if you are in a different application.

Select **Show Office Clipboard Icon on Taskbar** to display the clipboard icon at the bottom of your screen.

Choose **Show Status Near Taskbar When Copying** to display the status of a copied item on the taskbar.

Check each of the options you would like to enable from the list. Click a second time to disable the option.

Once the Office Clipboard has been activated, an icon 📋 will be placed on the Windows taskbar (notification tray) along the bottom right of your screen.

If you don't see the Office Clipboard icon on your taskbar, it may be one of the hidden items. Click on ⌃ to view the hidden items.

If you right-click or touch and hold (if using a touch screen) on the clipboard icon 📋 located along the taskbar at the bottom of your screen, the following list of options will be displayed:

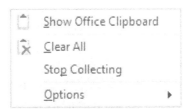

From this list, you can choose to display the Office Clipboard, clear all of the items currently being stored within the clipboard, or close the clipboard. The last item within this list allows you to specify the display options for the clipboard (which were discussed on the previous page).

If you do not specify otherwise, the collected items remain in the Clipboard until you close all Office applications.

ALIGNING CELL DATA

USAGE:

Unless you specify otherwise, Excel left-justifies text and right-justifies numbers so that text fills cell space from left to right while numbers are filled from right to left so that they align properly.

To change the horizontal cell alignment for a single cell or a group of selected cells, click or tap on one of the following tools (located within the Alignment section on the Home Ribbon):

≡ **Left**

≡ **Centered**

≡ **Right**

MERGE AND CENTER ACROSS COLUMNS

You can also merge a group of cells and then center a heading across the new cell. For example, if you have a title in cell A1 that you would like centered across several adjacent columns (they must be blank), you can have Excel automatically merge the cells and then center the data in that new cell.

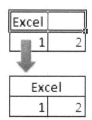

To merge and then center a group of cells, follow these two steps:

❶ Select both the cell containing the data and the empty adjacent cells in which you want to merge and center the information. Once selected, release the mouse button.

❷ Click or tap on the ⊞ Merge & Center ▾ tool (which is located within the Alignment section on the Home Ribbon).   If you select this tool a second time, Excel will remove the centering and place the data in the original cell.

VERTICALLY ALIGNING DATA

You can also align data vertically (top, center or bottom) within a cell or block of cells.

After selecting the cell(s) to be aligned, click or tap on one of the three tools shown below (which are located within the Alignment section on the Home Ribbon):

 Top

Center

Bottom

INDENTING TEXT WITHIN A CELL

You can indent text within a cell. This can help when creating lists or outlines.

After selecting the cell(s) to be indented/outdented, click or tap on one of the two tools shown below (which are located within the Alignment section on the Home Ribbon):

Click or tap this button to **indent** the current cell text.

Click or tap this tool to **outdent** the current cell text.

Each time you click or tap on one of these tools, Excel indents/outdents the cell(s) one more level.

CHANGING TEXT ORIENTATION

You can rotate text within a cell to a diagonal angle or vertical orientation. This can be useful when trying to label narrow columns.

Begin by selecting the cell(s) to be modified.

 Click or tap on the **Orientation** tool (which is located within the Alignment section on the Home Ribbon).

A list of orientation choices is displayed. Select the one you want to use.

If you select the same choice a second time, the cell(s) will revert back to the normal orientation.

WRAPPING TEXT WITHIN A CELL

If you have more text than fits horizontally within a cell and you don't want to widen the column to display it, you can choose to wrap the text within the cell.

Begin by selecting the cell(s) to be modified.

 Click or tap the **Wrap Text** tool (which is located within the Alignment section on the Home Ribbon).

Click or tap the tool a second time to remove the wrap text option.

FORMATTING NUMBERS

USAGE:

When entering values, Excel automatically uses a format which omits dollar signs, commas and a fixed number of decimal places. This can make numbers difficult to read at times and inconsistent. Excel does, however, allow you to access other built-in formats (such as percentage signs, dollar signs, etc.).

Select the cells to format and then choose one of the following tools (located within the Number section on the Home Ribbon):

Click or tap the down arrow ⊡ beside this tool (located within the Number section of the Home Ribbon) to choose from a list of formats.

$ ▾

Formats the current selection for **currency** with a dollar sign, a comma as a thousand separator and 2 decimal places. If you click or tap the down arrow ⊡ beside this tool, you can select which country's currency symbol to use. Example: **$45.00**

%

Formats the current selection for **percentage** by multiplying the numbers by 100 and adds the percent sign to the end with 0 decimal places. Example: **45%**

Instructor Note:

Allow students time to play with these options as you show them.

͵

Formats the selection for **comma** by adding a comma as a thousand separator and two decimal places. Example: **4,500.00**

←.0
.00

Increases the number of decimal places displayed. Each time this button is selected another decimal place is added to the selection.

.00
→.0

Decreases the number of decimal places displayed. Each time this button is selected another decimal place is removed from the selection.

INSERTING A ROW/COLUMN

USAGE:

As you work with a worksheet, you may find it necessary to add a row or column. When inserting, Excel will move the contents of the currently selected row down or the current column to the right to make room for the new row/column.

To insert a column or row, follow these steps:

❶ Select the row or column header where the new one should appear.

NOTE:	To insert more than one row or column, you will need to click and drag across multiple row/column headers to show how many you want to insert.

❷

Insert

While pointing to the selected column(s) or row(s), click or tap on this tool (located within the **Cells** section on the Home Ribbon).

The new column(s) or row(s) should have been inserted.

DELETING A ROW/COLUMN

USAGE:

You may also find yourself needing to delete a row or column.

Your first step will be to select the column or row to be removed.

To remove a column or row, follow the steps outlined below:

❶   The first step in deleting a row or column is to select it (using one of the methods described previously).

❷
Delete

While pointing to the selected column(s) or row(s), click or tap on this tool (located within the Cells section on the Home Ribbon).

The selected row(s) or column(s) will have been removed from the worksheet.

PRACTICE EXERCISE

Instructions:		
	❶	Open the **REGIONS** file.
	❷	Insert three rows at the top of the spreadsheet to add the title shown in the exercise below.
	❸	Insert a new column E for the quarterly objective (QTR OBJ) and enter the information as listed in the exercise below.
	❹	Figure out how much of the quarterly objective was reached (% OBJ) in column G and copy the formula down to the other cells within that column.
	❺	Format column B for dollar signs with 2 decimal points. Format column G for percentages with 0 decimal points. Columns C-F should be formatted for fixed with 2 decimal points.
	❻	Save the file and close it when you are done.

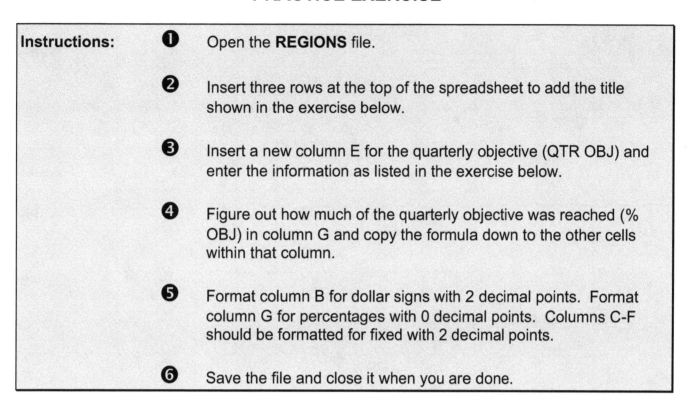

REGIONAL PART SALES
FOURTH QUARTER

REGION	OCT	NOV	DEC	QTR OBJ	QTR TOTAL	% OBJ
Pacific	$2.30	1.80	1.20	5.50	5.30	96%
Northwest	$1.60	1.10	.90	4.00	3.60	90%
Northeast	$2.50	2.20	2.00	6.00	6.70	111%
Gulf	$3.10	2.90	2.50	8.00	8.50	106%
Southeast	$2.60	2.10	1.80	6.00	6.50	108%

Module Four

- **Working with Function Arguments**

WORKING WITH FUNCTION ARGUMENTS

USAGE:

General mathematical functions are provided with Excel to carry out calculations on data within the spreadsheet and can take the place of certain types of formulas.

Functions begin with the **=** sign just as formulas do. For example, if you had a large column of numbers to be added (A1:A100), you might think you need a long formula to include all of the addresses (=A1+A2+A3....+A99+A100). However, Excel provides a mathematical function which is used primarily to add blocks of numbers. The formula could be re-written as **=SUM(A1:A100)** which is much shorter.

To calculate the sum of a block of numbers, move to the cell where the answer is to be placed and use this function argument:

=SUM(FIRST CELL:LAST CELL)

You must define the block just like any other block by specifying the first and last cell addresses.

To calculate the average value for a block of cells:

=AVERAGE(FIRST CELL:LAST CELL)

To return the largest value in a block of cells:

=MAX(FIRST CELL: LAST CELL)

To return the smallest value in a block of cells:

=MIN(FIRST CELL:LAST CELL)

To count the number of numeric entries in a block of cells:

=COUNT(FIRST CELL:LAST CELL)

WORKING WITH FUNCTION ARGUMENTS

If you would like some guidance, Excel can list the most common functions and then prompt you for the various arguments required by displaying the function arguments.

As soon as you type the 🗐 sign, this button will be listed along the left side of the Formula Bar. The last function you chose will be displayed on the button. If you click or tap on the button that function will be selected.

To choose a different function, click or tap the down arrow ⯆ to the right of the button and then select a new function from the list.

Once the function has been selected Excel will prompt you to enter the remaining arguments (cell addresses) for the function, as shown below:

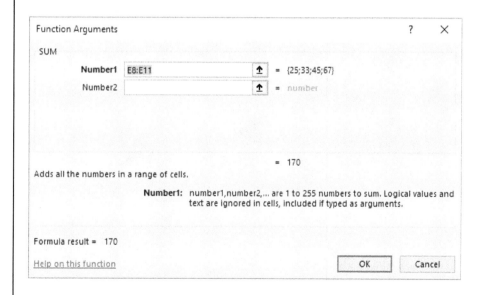

When you are done, select ⌈ OK ⌉.

Instructor Note:

Have students try the quick double-click method at the end of a column or row but also have them try summing a group of cells that are not together.

THE AUTOSUM FEATURE

Excel can make somewhat of an intelligent decision on its own and determine which cells of a row or column should be "summed". This is called the **AutoSum** feature.

To quickly add the contents of a column or row, follow the steps shown below:

❶   Select the cell either to the right or below the cells that are to be totaled.

❷   ∑ AutoSum ▾   **Double-Click** or **Double-Tap** on this tool (which is located within the Editing section on the Home Ribbon).

NOTE: *If you only click/tap on the AutoSum tool once, Excel will highlight the cells it assumes you want to include in the formula. The second click/tap is used to confirm the selection.*

If, by chance, Excel has selected the wrong group of cells, you can highlight the correct block before clicking/tapping on the tool a second time.

ACCESSING OTHER FUNCTIONS

In addition to adding a column or row, the AutoSum tool can also be used to perform a variety of other function arguments.

To access one of the other available functions, follow the steps outlined below:

❶   Select the cell where you want the function to be stored.

❷   Σ AutoSum ▾   Click or tap on the down arrow ☑ beside this tool (located within the Editing section on the Home Ribbon).

❸
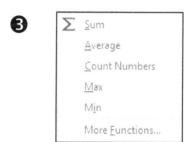
Excel will provide a pull-down list of the most commonly used functions.

Select the function you want to use from the list provided.

❹

If you look in the current cell, you will see that the function has been placed in the cell.

Σ AutoSum ▾ ▾   You will need to confirm that this is correct by clicking on the AutoSum tool a second time to accept the function.

> **NOTE:**   *If, by chance, Excel has selected the wrong group of cells, you can highlight the correct block before clicking on the tool a second time.*

To have Excel perform a function that is not displayed in the pull-down list, you will need to access the **Insert Function** dialog box, as outlined in the steps below:

❶   Be sure that the current cell is the one in which you want the function to be placed.

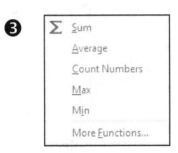

❷   Click or tap on the down arrow ▾ beside the **AutoSum** tool (located within the Editing section on the Home Ribbon).

❸   Excel will provide a pull-down list of the most commonly used functions.

Select **More Functions...** from the list provided.

The following dialog box will be displayed:

❹ The dialog box (displayed on the previous page) is divided into two main sections. The top section allows you to either enter key words/ short description of the type of function you need or select the type of function you are searching for by selecting one of the categories listed.

After entering the explanation or selecting the category, click or tap on [Go] to view a list of related functions.

The bottom of the dialog box lists the results of your search.

Select the function you want to use and click/tap [OK].

❺ You will be taken to a second dialog box where you will enter the block of cells to apply the function to, as shown below:

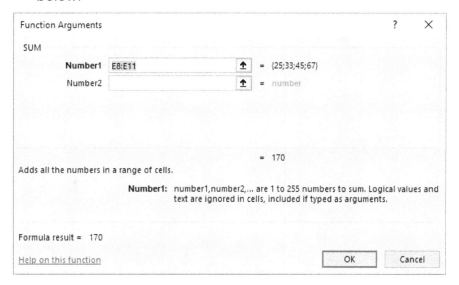

❻ Type the block of cells in the box provided or click back in the worksheet to highlight the desired cells.

If you click or tap on the ⬆ button (within in the "Function Arguments" dialog box), the dialog box will be collapsed and you will be returned to the worksheet where you can use the mouse to select the block for the function.

A bar will be displayed while you select the block of cells to include in the formula, as illustrated below:

Once you have selected or entered the block of cells to use for the function, re-activate the "Function Arguments" dialog box by clicking or tapping on the ⬇ button (located in the upper right corner of the bar).

❼   When done, choose OK or press the ENTER key.

PRACTICE EXERCISE

Instructions:	❶	Open the **REGIONS** file.
	❷	Create an area at the bottom of your spreadsheet to figure out the column totals and averages by month.
	❸	Save the file when you are done and close it.

REGIONAL PART SALES
FOURTH QUARTER

REGION	OCT	NOV	DEC	QTR OBJ	QTR TOTAL	% OBJ
Pacific	$2.30	1.80	1.20	5.50	5.30	96%
Northwest	$1.60	1.10	.90	4.00	3.60	90%
Northeast	$2.50	2.20	2.00	6.00	6.70	111%
Gulf	$3.10	2.90	2.50	8.00	8.50	106%
Southeast	$2.60	2.10	1.80	6.00	6.50	108%
Totals:	$12.10	10.10	8.40			
Averages:	$2.42	2.02	1.68			

Module Five

- Applying Attributes
- Working with Fonts
- Borders and Colors
- Adding Cell Shading
- Using Cell Styles

APPLYING ATTRIBUTES

USAGE:

Instructor Note:

This module is fun for students so allow plenty of time for them to play around.

As you enter and edit data, you can change its appearance to add emphasis and make the worksheet easier to read. To enhance a cell or group of cells you can either use the keyboard or the **Home Ribbon**. All of the character attributes are located within the "Font" section on this ribbon.

Select the cell or block of cells to be modified and then click on one of the following tools (which are located within the Font section on the Home Ribbon):

B	Click or tap this tool to turn **bold** on and off.
I	Click or tap this tool to turn *italics* on and off.
U ▾	Click or tap on this tool to turn underline on and off.
A ▾	Click or tap this tool to change the font color.
A˄ A˅	Use these tools to **increase**/decrease the font size.

If you prefer using the keyboard, select the cell(s) to be modified and then press one of the following shortcut keys:

CTRL + B	This key combination toggles **bold** on/off.
CTRL + I	This key combination toggles *italics* on/off.
CTRL + U	This key combination toggles underline on/off.

REMOVING ATTRIBUTES

If you decide you want to clear the attributes that have been applied to a cell or block of cells, you can quickly do so.

After selecting the cell(s) containing the attributes to be removed, click or tap the **Clear** tool (located within the Editing section on the Home Ribbon).

From the list, choose **Clear Formats**.

CHANGING FONTS & POINT SIZE

USAGE:

To make your workbook appear more interesting, you may want to change the font or apply different font sizes to titles or headings.

To change the font of a cell or block of selected cells, follow the steps outlined below:

❶ Select the cell(s) to be changed.

❷ Click or tap on the down arrow ⊡ beside the **Font** tool (which is located within the Font section on the Home Ribbon).

Excel displays a preview of each font directly within the list. As you hover over each font, Excel will also preview that font within the currently selected cell(s) within the worksheet.

❸ Select the desired font from the pull-down list.

NOTE:	Notice that Excel displays the current theme fonts along with the last few selected fonts at the top of the list for easy access.
	Some fonts have a cloud icon beside them, indicating they must be downloaded.

CHANGING THE FONT SIZE

You can also easily change the size of the font that is applied to a cell or block of cells.

To change the font size, follow the steps outlined below:

❶   Select the cell(s) to be changed.

❷   11 ▾   Click or tap on the down arrow ⊡ beside the **Font Size** button (which is located within the Font section on the Home Ribbon).

❸   Select the desired point size from the pull-down list.

You can also use the following tools (both of which are located within the Font section on the Home Ribbon) to quickly increase or decrease the font size.

A˄   A˅   Click or tap on these tools to quickly increase or decrease the current font size.

Instructor Note:

Explain that these two tools are great for visually seeing the font grow/shrink when you aren't sure how large or small you want to go.

CELL BORDERS AND COLORS

USAGE:

Excel also allows you to add borders to your cell entries. Lines and boxes provide useful visual emphasis for important information in a worksheet. With borders, you can create custom forms.

ADDING CELL BORDERS

 Select the cell(s) to apply the border to.

❷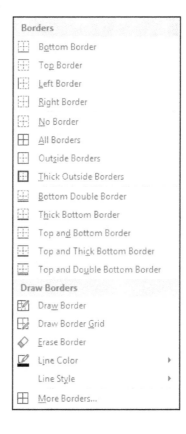

Click or tap on the down arrow ▾ beside the **Borders** tool (located within the Font section on the Home Ribbon).

❸ From the pull-down list, choose the type of border to be applied to the selected block of cells.

If you choose the options toward the bottom of the list (labeled **Draw Borders**), you can manually draw and erase borders using the drawing tools.

ADDING A FILL COLOR

You can also choose to add a background color to the selected cell(s) when working with color displays or printouts.

❶ Select the cell(s) to fill.

❷

Click or tap on the down arrow ▾ to the right of the **Fill Color** tool (which is located within the Font section on the Home Ribbon). Excel will display a palette of available colors from which to choose.

Notice you can choose to have no fill color.

❸ From the pull-down list, choose the fill color to be applied to the selected block of cells.

CHANGING THE FONT COLOR

Although Excel defaults to printing in black, if you have a color printer you can change the color of the font by accessing the Home Ribbon, as shown in the steps below:

❶

Click or tap this tool to use the last selected color or click on the down arrow ⊡ beside the **Font Color** tool (located within the Font section on the Home Ribbon) to choose another font color.

❷ Select the color you want to use (from the pull-down list) for the selected text.

NOTE:	*The color you chose last becomes the default. If you look at the tool, the current color will be shown (as an underline for the letter A on the tool).*

CUSTOMIZING CELL FORMATS

USAGE:

You may decide you would like to further customize the number formats, borders, fonts, shading or alignment.

To do this, follow these steps:

❶ Select the block of cells you want to modify and then click your **[RIGHT]** mouse button or tap and hold (if using a touch screen device).

❷

From the pop-up menu that is displayed, select **Format Cells...**

| NOTE: | You can also access these options by clicking or tapping on the dialog box launcher from the Font, Alignment or Number sections on the Home Ribbon. |

THE NUMBER TAB

If the cell you have selected is numeric, you will see the following dialog box:

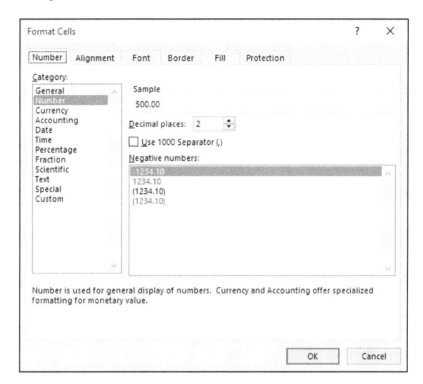

This first tab is used to choose the format to apply to numbers.

Along the left side of the dialog box is a section labeled **Category**. Scroll through the list until you find the desired category (e.g., currency, percentage, date, time).

Depending on the category selected, the right side of the dialog box displays additional formatting information. For example, if you select **Currency**, the right side allows you to specify the symbol to be used (**$**), how many decimal places to display and how negative numbers should be shown.

To customize the current setting, use the right side of the dialog box to make the necessary changes.

A sample of the currently selected format is displayed at the top of the dialog box.

THE ALIGNMENT TAB

The second tab determines the alignment of the selected cells.

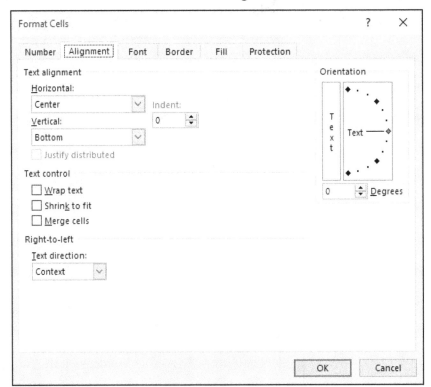

Horizontal	Determines the horizontal alignment of cell text (from the left and right sides of the cell).
Vertical	Determines the vertical alignment of cell text (from the top and bottom edges of the cell).
Orientation	Sets the orientation of the cell(s). Drag the orientation marker to specify the exact degree setting or click on the vertical text box to change the character orientation to vertical.
Text control	The first checkbox within this section determines whether long cell entries should be wrapped within the cell. The second shrinks the font of the selected cell(s) to fit the column width. The last box merges selected cells to a single cell.
Right-to-left	Click or tap the down arrow ˅ beside this option to specify the selected cells' text direction.

THE FONT TAB

This tab is used to change the font and attributes.

Font	Lists available fonts to choose from.
Font style	Adds attributes, such as bold and italics.
Size	Sets the point size.
Underline	Sets the type (if any) of underlining to apply.
Color	Selects the font color.
Normal font	Returns to the default font settings.
Effects	Toggles super/subscript/strikethrough on/off.
Preview	Previews the changes as you make them.

THE BORDER TAB

This tab allows you to select one of Excel's preset borders or customize your own.

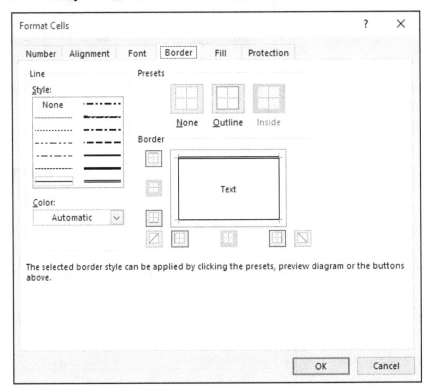

Line Style	Use this section to choose one of the line styles to be applied to the border. Click on the style for your customized border.
Presets	After choosing a line style, use this top section to select one of the preset borders available within Excel.
Color	This section is used to change the color of the selected border. Click or tap on the down arrow ⌄ beside this option to select the color for your customized border.
Border	Use this section to create your own customized borders by first choosing the border style and color (from the left side of the dialog box) and then clicking in the area provided to actually define the borders.

THE FILL TAB

This tab is used to choose the cell shading color and pattern to be applied to the selected cell(s).

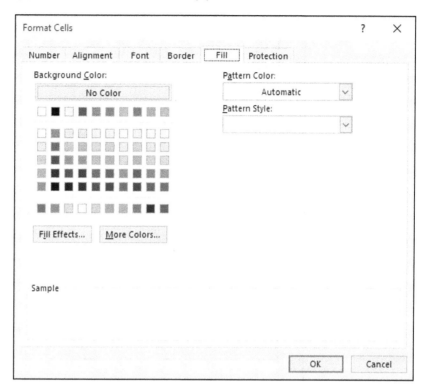

Background Color   Selects the color to be applied as shading. Click or tap on the color from the palette provided in this section. There are two buttons beneath this section which allow you to specify fill effects or select from a complete color palette. Be sure to choose a color that allows the text to be easily read.

Pattern Color   Selects the pattern color. Click or tap on the down arrow ∨ beside this option to select a custom pattern.

Pattern Style   Selects the pattern style to be applied. Click or tap on the down arrow ∨ beside this option to select a custom style.

Sample   Displays the changes as you make them.

THE PROTECTION TAB

This tab is used to specify how the selected cell(s) or objects will be handled when the worksheet is protected.

Locked	By default, all cells are locked when the sheet is protected. If this box is unchecked, the next time the worksheet is protected the selected cell(s) or graphic objects can still be modified.
Hidden	If this box is checked, the next time the worksheet is protected the selected cell(s) will have their formulas hidden.

❸ Use the six tabbed boxes discussed above to customize the selected block of cells as desired.

❹ After making the customization changes, click or tap on OK to save the changes, close the dialog box and return to your worksheet.

USING CELL STYLES

USAGE:

Cell Styles apply a set of predefined formats to a block of cells. These can include fonts, borders, patterns, alignment, and shading.

To apply a cell style to a block of cells, follow these steps:

❶ Select the block of cells to be modified.

❷ Select the desired **Cell Style** from the list provided (located within the Styles section on the Home Ribbon).

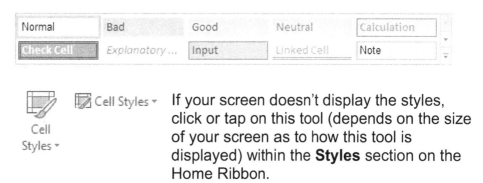

If your screen doesn't display the styles, click or tap on this tool (depends on the size of your screen as to how this tool is displayed) within the **Styles** section on the Home Ribbon.

The following list of styles will be displayed:

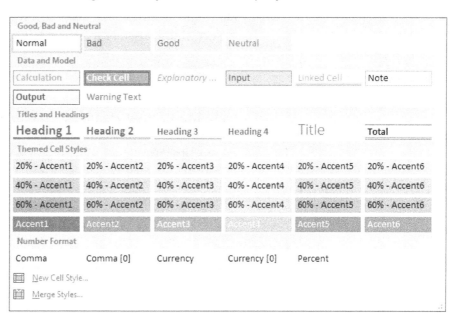

Instructor Note:

Explain that Excel's built-in styles allow you to quickly format a group of cells to make your workbook appear more professional.

Be sure to give students ample time to play with several styles.

❸ Scroll through the list until you find the one you want to apply to the selected block. Notice you can create a new cell style yourself or merge styles contained within another workbook.

USING THE FORMAT PAINTER

USAGE:

Excel offers a feature which allows you to copy attributes from one block of cells and apply them to another block. This feature can save you time by quickly copying the format of a block of cells.

To use the format painter feature, follow these steps:

❶   Select the cells containing the attributes to be copied.

❷   🖌 Format Painter   Select the Format Painter tool from the Home Ribbon. By default, it will only change one set of cells. If you plan on formatting more than one block of text, double-click or double-tap on this tool.

         ⬦🖌 Your mouse pointer changes to a paintbrush.

❸   Highlight the block of cells to be formatted. Excel will automatically apply the same formatting options you copied.

❹   If you had double-clicked or double-tapped the tool to begin with, the Format Painter remains active until you deactivate it by clicking/tapping the tool again. If you had only clicked/tapped the tool once, Excel automatically deactivates this feature after the first block is formatted.

PRACTICE EXERCISE

Instructions:	❶	Open the **REGIONS** file.
	❷	Add the borders and lines as shown below. Shade the totals and averages section at the bottom.
	❸	Bold the column headings and change the font to something larger for the first two title lines of the file.
	❹	When you are done save the file.

REGIONAL PART SALES
FOURTH QUARTER

REGION	**OCT**	**NOV**	**DEC**	**QTR OBJ**	**QTR TOTAL**	**% OBJ**
Pacific	$2.30	1.80	1.20	5.50	5.30	96%
Northwest	$1.60	1.10	.90	4.00	3.60	90%
Northeast	$2.50	2.20	2.00	6.00	6.70	111%
Gulf	$3.1	2.9	2.5	8.0	8.5	106%
Southeast	$2.60	2.10	1.80	6.00	6.50	108%
Totals:	$12.10	10.10	8.40			
Averages:	$2.42	2.02	1.68			

Module Six

- **Creating and Editing Charts**

CREATING A CHART

USAGE:

You can present worksheet data more effectively and make it easier to understand and analyze if you display it graphically, as illustrated below:

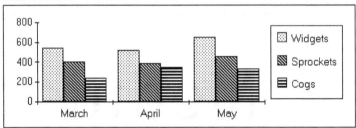

Monthly Sales Report

	March	April	May	3-Month Total
Widgets	546	522	653	1721
Sprockets	400	390	460	1250
Cogs	240	350	330	920

Instructor Note:

Charts are covered in depth in future classes but it's important that students leave the beginning class understanding how to create a chart from their data and how to format it.

To quickly create a chart, follow these steps:

❶   Select the data to be included within the chart.

❷   Switch to the **Insert** Ribbon.

❸   From within the section labeled **Charts**, select a chart category (column, line, pie, bar, area or scatter).

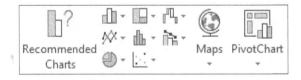

❹   A pull-down list of available chart types will be displayed. Each chart type (column, pie, scatter, etc.) includes a down arrow ▾ to show all available charts within that category. Select the exact chart type from this list or scroll the "**Recommended Charts**" to have Excel show you a preview of the best type of chart for your selected data.

Once you have selected a chart type, Excel will create the chart based on the data in the cells you selected and the type of chart you have chosen:

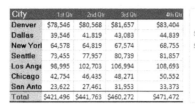
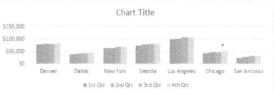

SELECTING CHART OBJECTS

Before you can modify any chart object, you must first select the chart (by clicking or tapping on it once) and then clicking/tapping on the object within the chart that you wish to modify.

SIZING THE CHART

❶ Click or tap on any of the outside borders surrounding the chart. Be sure you see the circles/handles around the chart.

❷ Point to one of the handles. Mouse users will see the pointer change to a double-sided arrow.

❸ Click/tap and drag the handle to resize the chart.

MOVING THE CHART

It is also possible to move the chart to a new location within the worksheet. You move a chart by selecting it and then dragging it to its new location.

❶ Select the outside border of the chart. Be sure you see the handles surrounding the chart.

❷ Point to one of the outside borders. Mouse users will see the pointer change to a four-way arrow. Click or tap and then drag the chart to its new location.

Instructor Note:

Be sure that students see the difference between clicking on the background of the chart (which allows them to move the entire chart as one piece) and clicking on a single chart item (which is used to edit that item).

EDITING THE CHART

Once the chart has been added to your worksheet, you can edit it using the ribbon across the top of your screen and the three new tools that appear to the right of the selected chart:

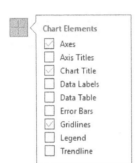

The **Chart Elements** tool allows you to add, remove or change the titles, axes, legend, gridlines and data labels. The number of items within this list will vary depending on the type of chart.

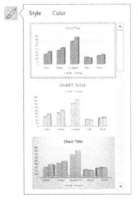

The **Chart Styles** tool is used to apply styles and define a color scheme for the selected chart.

The **Chart Filters** tool defines what values within the worksheet are being displayed within the chart.

PRINTING THE CHART

Once you add the chart to your worksheet, you can either print the chart by itself or as part of the sheet. If the chart is not selected, it will be printed as an object along with your cell data.

To print the chart alone, click or tap on it once (to select it) and then follow the normal printing steps.

❶  Click or tap the **File Tab** on the Ribbon Bar.

❷ Select **Print** from the pull-down list.

Only the chart will be printed.

Instructor Note:

Since these are the same tools students used to format text, this section should go quickly.

APPLYING TEXT ATTRIBUTES TO CHART OBJECTS

You can quickly apply attributes to chart objects the same way you applied attributes to cell contents.

Select the portion of the chart to be modified and then click or tap on one of the following tools (which are located within the Font section on the Home Ribbon):

B   Click or tap this tool to turn **bold** on and off.

I   Click or tap this tool to turn *italics* on and off.

U ▾   Click or tap this tool to turn <u>underline</u> on and off.

CHANGING THE FONT OF CHART OBJECTS

You can change the font of a chart object just as you would any other cell.

Before continuing, select the chart object to modify.

❶   Click or tap on the down arrow ⊡ beside the **Font** tool (located within the Font section on the Home Ribbon).

❷

Click or tap on the down arrow ⊡ beside the **Font** tool (which is located within the Font section on the Home Ribbon).

Excel displays a preview of each font directly within the list. As you hover over each font, Excel will also preview that font within the currently selected cell(s) within the selected item in the chart.

CHANGING FONT SIZE

To quickly change the font size of an object on your chart, select the object and then click on the down arrow beside the **Font Size** tool (located within the Font section on the Home Ribbon). From the list provided, select the new size.

If you are unsure of the exact size you would like to select, you can use the following tools to incrementally change the font size:

A^ A˅   Click or tap on these tools to quickly increase or decrease the current font size.

CHANGING THE FONT COLOR

Although Excel defaults to printing text in black, you can quickly change the color of the font by selecting the text object and then accessing the tool bar, as shown below:

❶   Click or tap on this tool (located within the Font section on the Home Ribbon).

❷   Select the color you want to use (from the pull-down list) for the selected text.

CHANGING COLORS

You may also want to change the colors of one of the data series on the chart.

❶   Select the data series (set of bars) you want to fill.

❷      Click or tap on the down arrow ▾ to the right of the **Fill Color** tool. Excel will display a palette of available colors from which to choose.

Notice you can remove the existing fill color from the selected object by choosing the option labeled "No Fill".

PRACTICE EXERCISE

Instructions:	❶	Open the **REGIONS** file. Delete the row with the **GULF** data.
	❷	Create a 3-D column chart based on the sales data from the worksheet using the data for Oct, Nov & Dec.
	❸	Add a chart title as shown in the example below.
	❹	Edit the chart to change the font for the title to something larger. Change the patterns of the columns. Add a legend.
	❺	When done, save the worksheet with the embedded chart.

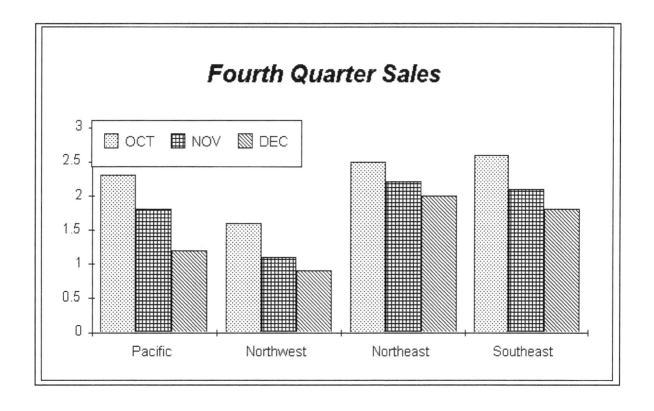

If You Have Time

- **Absolute Cell Addressing**
- **The Quick Analysis Tool**
- **Working with Templates**

ABSOLUTE CELL ADDRESSING

USAGE:

During the copy procedure, Excel adjusts formulas depending on the cell(s) the formulas are copied to, thus ensuring that the formulas being copied appropriately refer to other locations on the spreadsheet. This is referred to as **relative** addressing since the cell addresses of a formula adjust "relative" to their new position.

There may be instances, however, when you may not want the formulas to be adjusted according to the cell(s) they are copied to. For example, if you have a list of salaries and want to uniformly increase those salaries by a percentage (5%), you would multiply the current salaries by the cell containing the 5%. All salaries would need to be multiplied by that one cell.

When creating a formula to calculate new salaries, that cell would, then, be referred to as **absolute**, meaning that no matter how many times you copied the formula down a column or across a row that particular cell address would not change within the formula.

Excel uses the dollar sign ($) to signify that a cell is absolute. For example, to make cell C2 absolute you would enter **C2** within the formula. By placing dollar signs before the column and again before the row, you are indicating that both the column and row are to be absolute (never adjusted when copied).

Below are examples of how the dollar signs can be used depending on which portion of the cell address should be absolute and which portion should remain relative.

C2	Column C is relative, row 2 is relative
$C2	Column C is absolute, row 2 is relative
C$2	Column C is relative, row 2 is absolute
C2	Column C is absolute, row 2 is absolute

If the 5% mentioned in the example above was in cell C2 and the first salary affected was in cell B3, the formula to calculate the new salary would be:

=(B3*C2)+B3

You would, then, copy the formula as needed. After doing this, notice that B3 is adjusted after being copied but cell C2 never is.

USING THE QUICK ANALYSIS TOOL

USAGE:

It used to take work to analyze your data, but now it only takes a few steps. You can instantly create different types of charts, including line and column charts, or add miniature graphs (called sparklines) to your worksheets. You can also apply a table style, create PivotTables, quickly insert totals, and apply conditional formatting. Although most of these items are discussed in more advanced workshops, it's important to at least know that these features exist and are very simple to access.

To use this feature, follow the steps outlined below:

❶ Select the cells to be included.

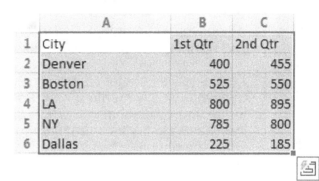

❷ Click or tap on the ⊡ button (located in the bottom right corner of the selected cells).

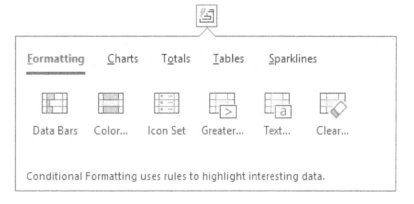

❸ There are five tabs within the Quick Analysis gallery. For example, choose Charts to see your selected data in one of the available charts. Pick an option, or just point to each one to see a preview of your data.

WORKING WITH TEMPLATES

USAGE:

Excel's **Template** feature allows you to create master workbooks with standard information or calculations. Rather than creating new workbooks from scratch each time, a template file can be set up to save you time. Templates can consist of text, calculations, and/or formatting codes.

For example, the format for your company invoices could be stored as a template for easy access. The template would consist of the logos, formatting, and formulas that don't change from one invoice to another. Whenever you need a new invoice you could simply create a new workbook based on your own invoice template and then simply enter the new information.

There are several built-in templates which you may use to create invoices, purchase orders, and other business workbooks.

Whenever you create a new workbook, Excel asks which template you would like to use. The default is a blank workbook.

Template files contain the extension **.XLTX**. To create your own template, simply create a new workbook, enter the data and formatting codes that you would like stored with the template and then save the file as a template rather than the usual workbook. Once the template has been saved, you may create new workbooks based on your template.

Each time you create a new workbook based on a template, Excel creates a new workbook (untitled until you save it) but places all of the text and/or calculations in that file based on the template.

Excel needs to know what folder your personal templates will be stored in before you can create a new document based on your templates.

Instructor Note:

Explain that most users do not have the time or design skills to make their workbooks look professional.

Excel understands that and includes templates which allow you to apply professional looking formats to your workbooks.

Everyone likes this section so be sure to cover it fully.

DEFINING YOUR TEMPLATE FOLDER

To define the location of your templates, follow these steps:

❶ Select **Options** from the pull-down list of items within the File tab on the Ribbon.

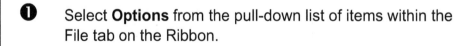

❷ Select the **SAVE** option (along the left).

The following dialog box will be displayed:

❸ Click or tap in the box labeled **Default personal templates location** and enter the exact location (drive and folder) where you will be storing your templates.

> **NOTE:** *Since there's unfortunately no* Browse... *button in this box to search your system for the folder, you'll need to know the exact path yourself. A solution could be clicking or tapping the* Browse... *button on the box labeled "Server drafts location" locate the path and then copy and paste it in this box.*

❹ When done, click or tap OK .

CREATING A NEW TEMPLATE

The simplest method for defining a new template is to create a workbook as you would any other and then save it as a template.

After creating the workbook and inserting all of the necessary information for the template, follow the steps outlined below to save it as a template for future workbooks to be based on:

 ❶   Select **Save As** from the pull-down list of options within the File tab on the Ribbon.

The following dialog box will be displayed:

❷   Select a folder or click on 📁 Browse

❸   In the resulting dialog box (shown below), click or tap on the down arrow ∨ beside the **Save as type** option and select "Excel Template (*.xltx)". Excel will automatically store the template in the folder you have defined as the location for templates.

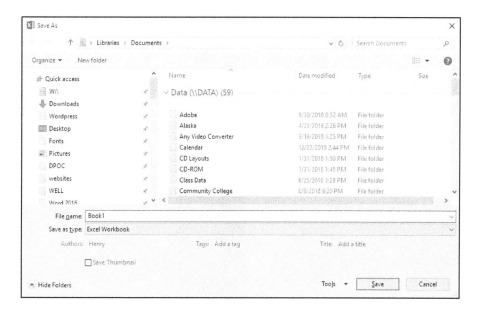

❹   Be sure you have entered a descriptive name for the template before clicking or tapping the [Save] button.

USING A TEMPLATE

To use the template that you created, you will follow the usual steps to create a new workbook with one exception. You will choose your template as the one to base the new workbook on.

To create a new workbook based on an existing template, follow the steps outlined below.

 Select **New** from the pull-down list of options within the File tab on the Ribbon.

The following window will be displayed:

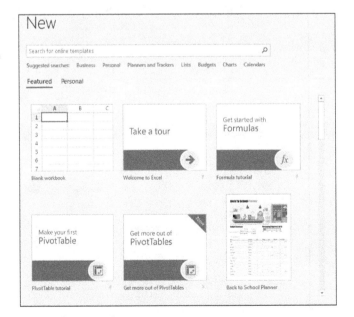

❷ Notice that Excel automatically displays the **Featured** templates (those created by Microsoft).

Select **Personal** (from the top of the window) as the type of templates to be displayed.

❸ Excel will change to display your personal templates. Select the one you wish to use by double-clicking or double-tapping on it.

A new workbook will be created – using the formatting defined in the selected template.

Instructor Note:

Have students open their template, make a change to it, save it and then create a new file based on the template to see the change.

EDITING A TEMPLATE

If you realize that a template needs to be modified, you can open it as you would any other workbook.

Once opened, you will be able to edit the template and then save it again.

Appendices

- **Appendix A: Function Keys**
- **Appendix B: Movement Keys**
- **Appendix C: Shortcut Keys**

APPENDIX A: FUNCTION KEYS

FUNCTION KEY		SHIFT	ALT	CTRL
F1	Help		New Chart	Display/Hide Ribbon
F2	Edit Cell	Edit a Comment	Save As	Print Preview
F3	Paste Name	Paste Function		Define Name
F4	Repeat		Exit Excel	Close Workbook
F5	Goto	Find		Restore Window Size
F6	Next Pane	Previous Pane		Next Workbook
F7	Spelling			Move Workbook
F8	Extend on/off	Add Mode on/off	Display Macros	Size Window
F9	Calculate All Sheets	Calculate Current Sheet		Minimize Workbook
F10	Menu	Shortcut Menu		Maximize Workbook
F11	New Chart	Insert Worksheet	Visual Basic Editor	New Macro Sheet
F12	Save As	Save		Open File

APPENDIX B: CURSOR MOVEMENT KEYS

KEYS:	ACTION:
CTRL + **←**	Moves to beginning of current block
CTRL + **→**	Moves to end of current block
CTRL + **↑**	Moves to top of current block
CTRL + **↓**	Moves to bottom of current block
HOME	Beginning of row
END + **→**	End of row
CTRL + **HOME**	Top left corner of worksheet
CTRL + **END**	Bottom right of worksheet (end of data)
PG↑	Moves up one screen
PG↓	Moves down one screen
ALT + **PG↑**	Moves left one screen
ALT + **PG↓**	Moves right one screen

APPENDIX C: SHORTCUT KEYS

KEYS:	ACTION:
CTRL + A	Select All
CTRL + B	Bold
CTRL + C	Copy
CTRL + F	Find
CTRL + H	Find & Replace
CTRL + I	Italics
CTRL + K	Insert a Hyperlink
CTRL + N	New Workbook
CTRL + O	Open a File
CTRL + P	Print
CTRL + S	Save
CTRL + U	Underline
CTRL + V	Paste
CTRL + W	Close Workbook
CTRL + X	Cut
CTRL + Y	Repeat Last Action
CTRL + Z	Undo